INVESTING OVER A CUP OF TEA

My not so profound thoughts on investing

NIMIT BRAHMBHATT

BOLD

An imprint of
Srishti Publishers & Distributors

Srishti Publishers & Distributors
A unit of AJR Publishing LLP
212A, Peacock Lane
Shahpur Jat, New Delhi – 110 049

editorial@srishtipublishers.com

First Published by Bold,
an imprint of Srishti Publishers & Distributors in 2023

10 9 8 7 6 5 4 3 2 1

This is a work of non-fiction, based on the author's experiences and life-learning. It provides practical solutions to everyday finance-related planning, but the recommendations given herein are in no way intended to be a substitute for professional advice and help.

Printed and bound in India

I want to dedicate this book to my parents
– my father, Gaurang Brahmbhatt
and my mother, Ketna Brahmbhatt.

Both of them have forced me to learn
and acquire new skills and even do
experiments in business,
and made me wise.

Contents

ACKNOWLEDGMENTS

I want to acknowledge my parents, as I have dedicated this book to them and my friends – Neil Shah, Aashirwad Patel and Harsh Desai, who are from engineering backgrounds and have helped me understand the complexities of the technologies and the functioning of different industries. Otherwise, my knowledge about the industry or the business would have been limited to just financial statements and not understanding the companies as they are.

I would especially like to thank Snehal sir and Suvas Barot (*mama*) who made me understand the investor mentality and helped me develop the same.

My uncles (mama), Vishal Barot, Keyur Barot and Aman Barot, gave me different perspectives to the same event. They even made me understand the consequences of certain actions or decision which impacted various businesses, which I was earlier not giving too much importance to.

I would also like to thank Anubhav Chaturvedi, who explained to me the concept of *ROHAS* and gave me a better understanding of the blockchain technology and its workings.

Lastly, I have my friends – Advait Rawal, Ronik Patel, Priyanka Maheshwari – and teachers, especially Satya sir, Mayank sir and Snehal sir from my Master's, who have provided me with different industry insights and made me understand how the corporates work.

Preface

Investing Over a Cup of Tea has been written to educate about the investment ideology, famous investors and how the masters of their fields use to generate wealth. The book focuses on long-term investment and the principles I have developed to avoid making mistakes while generating wealth.

I was always intrigued by how the stock markets work, and while growing up, I understood that a very few people could give good investment advice around me. Most of them didn't know about the company in detail, but were advising us to invest in the shares listening to others or from the past experiments they did with their investments.

While doing my Master's from EDII[1], I started my business in the packaging industry with a firm called Nimbus Corporation. I found out that most of the investors don't have accurate knowledge about investing in stock markets and have very little financial literacy.

Thus, I started with a blog and podcast and soon came up on YouTube, explaining all relevant finance-related topics.

While doing all this, I thought I must write a book which could reach a wider audience and give them a proper method to invest in different financial instruments and to educate further. I, Aashirwad and Harsh started an EdTech platform to work on closing the gap between the industry and what is being taught, as well as provide practical knowledge by bringing industry's experts.

1. EDII - Entrepreneurship Development Institute of India

How to read this book?

To have a clear understanding of the message or the ideology which I am conveying through this book, do read the book, chapter wise and if you have some knowledge regarding investing, you can read the Principles chapter in the beginning, in between or as it is given.

Why this book is relevant to you?

You might be thinking about this question. This book explains how a common man can invest in different stocks. How the mix of value investing taught by Benjamin Graham, Warren Buffet, and the investment philosophy of Peter Lynch and Rakesh Jhunjhunwala are mixed for the Indian marketplace. By understanding long-term ideology and how with very less analysis, one can look into future and understand which companies would grow over a period of ten to fifteen years and still be prevalent in the market. The book helps you to identify your investment style and makes you a better investor, one step at a time.

Regards
Nimit Brahmbhatt

1
Introduction

Even though it is quite an unusual name for an investment book, this is where most Indians discuss investment, job prospects, wealth creation and other stuff. You might also have discussed it with your friends over a cup of tea.

I look at the retail investors such as us – who earn less and invest a small portion of it; sometimes it might be 10% of the total income or more or even less. In this book, I will discuss investing in stock markets and the trend going on in investing in startups and opening new businesses.

I have covered different things which investors are looking for, such as cryptocurrencies and the functioning of technology, as well as my belief in investing in climate change. You may have seen or heard about the climate change summit and investments in renewable energy, which many firms are making in order to cut carbon emissions and move towards a more sustainable way of doing business. Thus, people in finance keep on bringing new terms such as the ESG Fund.

For all those investors who might not have heard the term ESG fund, it is something wherein the fund is created to look at three things:

1. Environment
2. Sustenance
3. Governance

Also, in this book, I will be discussing my investing approach, wherein I use a mix of value investing being used by Warren Buffet, as well as other combinations of investing used by Peter Lynch and other portfolio managers. You will see how I have been able to get results by using a combination approach, as only one approach won't be useful for the Indian audience or the Indian investors.

I will also discuss climate change as an option for investment, how that will be the future, and how by doing small research, one can earn great returns even though one is an amateur and doesn't know many things regarding stock markets and other investment decisions.

Once upon a time

Once upon a time… I went to the Angel Broking conference for the first time in 2006-2007, when I was in sixth grade, and it was my first interaction with the financial world of stock markets. I was taught how to apply common sense, and one could invest in promising companies and not worry about it.

The *mantra* was simple – look around yourself and identify stocks. I don't remember the fund manager's name, but it was the lesson in the form of his story. While he used MRF Tyres as an example, the stock was approximately Rs 8000 per share in October 2007, as I investigated while drafting the book, and it was during that time that he mentioned the share price. While the fund manager was researching, he used to travel a lot as they were required to look into things. The manager used to ask the taxi drivers which tyres they used? And at that time, most of them said that they used

MRF tyres. Considering this thing, he started looking around the different things which we own in general life. Such as, most people might be wearing watches from Tata company, wearing clothes from Pantaloons, Louis Philippe which is owned by Aditya Birla, or if you are eating in Domino's, you are consuming the product from Jubilant FoodWorks Ltd. There are even local companies, or we can say home grown brands, which are growing and giving competition to the MNCs. They might not be listed on the stock exchanges, but if we start observing the home grown brands and how the MNCs are growing, we might be able to understand the industries which are growing and stay away from all those industries which are not able to compete with the world.

Once we start looking at things in such a way, it would be much easier to eliminate bad companies. It was the single most important lesson I took from him and still apply when buying shares. While other things went above my head at that time, I still utilize the story and tell everyone who asks for advice, and you know the price as of now and can see the difference yourself.

Patience is the key

Patience is the key to winning this game. While I have seen many people trading daily, it seems nothing less than gambling. Most people forget that they are investing in a business, and it takes time for companies to grow big.

From a longer-term perspective, I still believe that for companies to showcase longer-term changes, the difference is usually seen in 10-15 years and not in 1-3 years. For example, when you start a business, it will take time to nurture. Then over a period of about fifteen years, you will see the actual difference in how much it has changed. Just because we can quickly sell it and purchase it doesn't mean we have to do it like others. Any investor must understand why they are investing in that particular company. If they don't know that, then I am pretty sure they will sell when the stock turns down.

Most of the time, even the peers who suggested us, don't know why they own a company and don't believe in longer-term, but just want some amount of profit and move out of it.

As I mentioned earlier, during Oct 2007 the price of MRF was Rs 8000.

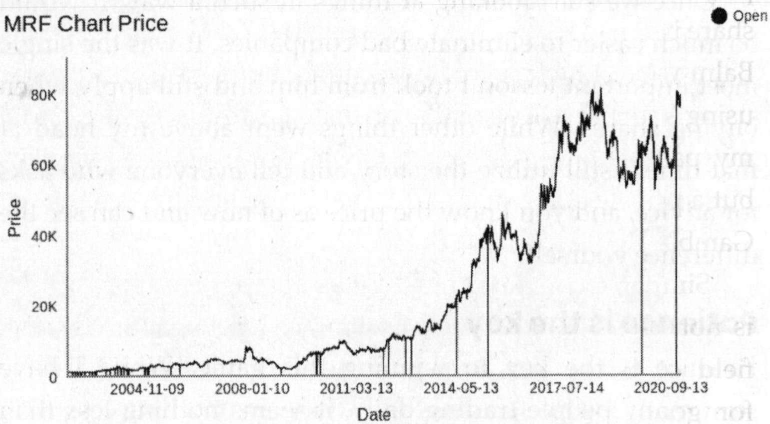

Image Source: Data from Yahoo Finance[2]

2 The MRF chart is just for reference to what happens when the company is good, and you remain invested for a longer time horizon.

So now you have understood how waiting for some ten years would generate returns for you moving to around 78-80K per share. MRF is not the only stock you see in your day-to-day life; there are many such as Titan, Asian Paints, HDFC, HDFC Bank, Exide, Amara Raja, Hero, Bajaj and the list goes on and on.

Is this a limited company?

This is where the investors need not just see things, but even observe. We mainly look at the companies with a good brand name, but have we looked at those companies we use regularly?

Every time in winter, many of us would get cold. All I see is Vicks VapoRub and very little competition from other players such as Amrutanjan, which have gained quite a good share in the market. I won't be applying Zandu Balm or Tiger Balm when I have a cold and cough, but I will definitely be using Vicks VapoRub or Amrutanjan. I was discussing it with my parents and saw that this was not a limited company but a private one, which is ultimately owned by Proctor and Gamble Hygiene & Healthcare Ltd.

Similarly, we have Tata Sky as another company which is not listed on the Stock Exchange. I belong to the same field of Cable and Broadcasting and have been waiting for good companies like this that are not listed on the Stock Exchanges.

Luckily, many companies have provided us with good returns and are listed, and it is how we look at familiar companies. The good thing about familiar companies is that we are already doing an analysis of the firm, such as Domino's

Pizza India, owned by Jubilant Foods and Sunfeast biscuits and other products developed by ITC.

While growing up we tend to develop a sense of which companies are good and which are not, considering the taste of the food, quality of the food, if it is a hotel how is the service of that hotel, how is the staff behaving, are they upkeeping the hotel or not and many other things. So why wait for our broker to give us advice whether the familiar company is good or not; you have already experienced it.

The tenbaggers

I have learnt this word from Peter Lynch, and I like using this word. It is a Wallstreet parlance as mentioned by Peter Lynch in his book[3]. So, what are tenbaggers?

Tenbaggers are those stocks that multiply your money ten times in value, plus the dividends you are getting are altogether different. As I mentioned earlier, MRF Ltd. was Rs 8000 in October 2007 and it touched Rs 80000, somewhere around 2018. It came out to be a tenbagger.

There is also Adani Green Ltd., which turned out to be a tenbagger. It started at Rs 29.45 and is now trading at Rs 969.20, giving returns thirty-one times, even though there is a lot of asset play going on.

Considering you have invested money in multiple companies as we always do and considering an investment in climate change, you select Adani Green Energy Ltd., which got listed in 2018 in the stock exchanges. You would have multiplied your investment thirty-one times. It is not so often

3 Lynch, *One Up on Wall Street: How to use what you already know to make money in the market*, 2000.

that we keep on getting tenbaggers; five and fourbaggers are common even with great companies. It was the time when Adani Green was trading at around Rs 56 per share, and I bought few shares of it.

Buying these shares has an interesting story. After earning my master's degree, I was about to graduate from college and was thinking about making an investment in climate change that might pay off in twenty years. So, I told my father to invest in Adani Green, and he immediately refused that there wasn't any guarantee that the stock would go up because it had already come down from a bigger price hike. I don't remember the price, but I came to know that it was down. He lent me some money, and inspired me to take a risk if I was sure, and I did. To make him believe, I bought a few shares and then sold them at their highest.

Though I believe in long-term investing, it was the money given by my father so that I could invest into some business for trial basis and then take an exit from that investment when the money was to be invested in our business.This was my first investment in climate change and now that things are moving ahead, I think this is one of the industries wherein there will be next 1000 unicorns. I shall explain more and the theory that I hold in the upcoming chapter.

There are multiple companies who have given great returns over the years and also provided good dividends.

The next step

Finding a good company to invest in by looking here and there and observing the role it plays in your daily life, is the first step.The next step is to conduct some research to help you sort out various companies based on their industrial category such as Indigo Airlines from Jet Airways, Muthoot Finance from DHFL, HDFC Bank from Yes Bank and so on. The list keeps going, but it is essential to identify the good ones from the bad ones.

It is not that I have not failed in identifying good companies from bad; even I have my current account in Yes Bank and was stuck during the crisis period. I understood from day one that the central government won't let the bank go down because of a management issue.

Observing companies in daily life does not mean we keep on investing in every company for the products that are trending or hot products. The repercussions of the economic scenario must also be looked upon, as well as the political scenario concerning the product itself.

You might have also seen that there are parent companies and there are individual companies which are both listed on the stock markets, and this is just my observation that many a time, an individual stand-alone company tends to give better stock returns than the parent company. Let me share an example with you – Bajaj Finserv is the parent company of Bajaj Finance Ltd. and Bajaj Finserv Ltd., and both the companies are listed on stock exchanges.

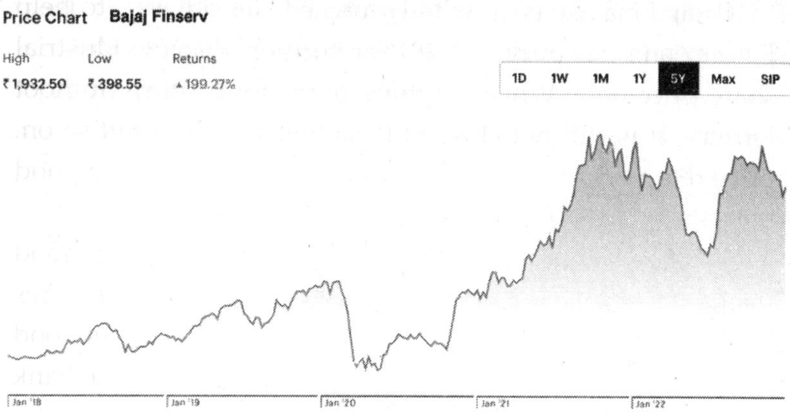

Image Source: Tickertape.in

The image shown above is of the parent company, Bajaj Finserv Ltd., which has given an absolute share price return of 199.27 % in the last five[4] years. While the total return considering the dividends would be more than 200%.

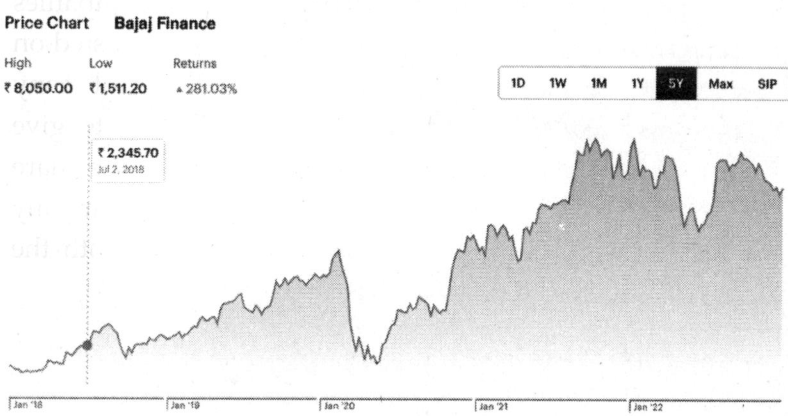

Image Source: Tickertape.in

4 Dt: 01/01/2023

Bajaj Finance is a wholly owned subsidiary of Bajaj Finserv and has provided 281% return on absolute basis on share price only. When we think of the total return by Bajaj Finserv, it is still not close to Bajaj Finance's absolute share price returns.

2.
INVESTING IN CLIMATE CHANGE

It was during school time that I watched a movie called *An Inconvenient Truth* wherein it was all about scientific explanation of what climate change is and how it will impact us in future. As I was pretty young at that time, it was difficult to understand the impacts that were happening as well as what would happen in future. Now, I am getting a hold of the severity and how an investor can benefit from it. But we must not forget one thing, the climate was changing even before humans arrived and is changing now, and it will keep on changing. It is a natural phenomenon wherein we are just adding fuel to fire and making the pace faster.

Multiple things are going on in the economy and the environment. How I look at things are majorly two categories. The first is ESG funds, and the second is the approach I have for finding out companies that would be investing in renewable energy, water, electricity, and other resources with sustainable development using top to bottom approach.

Top to bottom

It is a very simple approach wherein I look at the macro scenario and then narrow it down to micros.

Now for the understanding part, I usually invest in those companies wherein I have some idea of what the product is, how their business works and what will be the opportunities in future for the product and whether the same company would be there after twenty years or so.

Now for the sake of understanding, let me start with the Paris Climate change agreement, wherein countries have signed the agreement to reduce overall carbon emission and reach to zero carbon emissions goal. As India has also signed the agreement, there would definitely be demand for electric cars, electric two-wheelers, and EV charging stations. This is just narrowing for a certain point of view where Tata Motors have brought the electric vehicle and, many companies have started on a similar path, such as Mahindra and Mahindra, MG Motors, Kia Motors and many more companies.

The main thing for any electric company to be here would require the development of infrastructure of EV charging stations at multiple locations, which would not only enhance commercial vehicle sales, but would also be cutting cost for retail consumers as well as logistics companies. These are the direct beneficiary or the direct requirement for the same.

Now look at the materials required; the first thing would be batteries wherein companies such as Panasonic, Amara Raja, Exide Industries, Eveready, and other would be beneficiaries for the proposal. We might even see new startups coming up such as companies like Ola, Revolt, and many other, who are sourcing batteries from companies like Panasonic and Amara Raja and are assembling electric two wheelers. Even metal companies would be one of the major beneficiaries for the whole construction of EV infrastructure in the country.

Now, this is just one example of top to bottom approach; another segment we missed is renewables. The direct beneficiary of the renewables would be solar panel manufacturers, the servicing jobs and installation contractors, as well as companies producing windmills where they have long-term power purchase contracts with the government.

The next step is to look for companies with a good amount of market share and reputation, who would be able to capture the opportunity. You must have understood that I am a believer of investing in climate change and that is the reason I am writing a whole chapter on it. Let me tell you one thing, for the next 1000 unicorns all over the globe, the maximum would be in the ones in the renewable energy, or the companies focused on climate change to reduce emissions or doing something else. This is my assumption based on the macro factors which I am seeing. We have Ukraine-Russia war going on and the wrath is being faced by Europe because of energy crisis; even Brexit happened and after that the UK is faced with Prime Ministerial problems of not having a steady government till Rishi Sunak became the Prime Minister of UK.

Even though there was a lot of uncertainty, and he just became the PM, he was forced by the people even the members of his parliament to go to the Climate change summit and make certain contributions towards climate change and combatting climate change.

Opportunity in India

India has invested about $57 billion in climate change from 2014-19 and has created jobs directly or indirectly. Just imagine a situation in which we have so much to develop that in cities such as Mumbai, the residents have to park their vehicles on the road and have to pay for that parking facility made available to them; this has happened because of a lack of infrastructure. While we are paying so much for electricity, investing in wind farms/hydrogen projects and solar farms would reduce the overall cost of electricity and reduce carbon emissions to a great extent.

A report I read which McKinsey published, said that every $10 million investment in green energy would generate seventy-seven jobs as compared to the investment made in fossil fuels, which would generate approximately only twenty-five jobs.

Thinking of green investment has not only been a trend nowadays, but will also be the main thing of investing because sustainable investing is the key to the future; if we have a proper perspective as many implications happen because of climate change. Before I move on, understand that I am looking and estimating, or we can say assuming that these would be the probable changes that I see in the next 20-40 years coming from now.

There are multiple implications which happen due to climate change, such as increased heat stress on humans. I don't know if you are noticing or not, but the weather is going towards extremes, while there are heavy rainfalls, uneven rainfall that might happen without its season also increasing temperature which is changing the consumption pattern of the humans. At the same time, we opt for AC homes and cars, but do not think of rainwater harvesting and planting trees as much as we are cutting them.

Even there is an increased stress on the assets we purchase, such as air conditioner might not work when the temperature goes above 45°C. The houses we build are being affected, the machineries which we use in business for production purposes will start facing extreme heat and this phenomenon is going to reduce the life of the machines.

There is an extreme need for cold chain logistics, but I would rather say a need for a cold chain ecosystem, because the shelf life of the products is being affected day by day, as well as the variation in temperatures, which would necessitate warehouses to support such changes in the climate so that once the season of purchasing a particular crop or product is over, things would be stored in such a way that they are not greatly affected by climate change. I have also seen an increased number of hurricanes and floods happening in metro cities and different areas of the country, which bring life to a pause and cause irreparable damage to the appliances as well as expenses to the family. A city such as Mumbai has started experiencing frequent floods, which will increase in the coming years. I was reading on climate central that by 2050, land that is currently home to almost thirty lakh people will fall below the elevation of coastal flood.

What we have seen during the pandemic is just a trailer, but there can be a shortage of food and water. I read that South Africa came near zero water day and even Chennai in India. Such extreme events and increasing population might result in a drought-like situation in many parts of the country, which might start a civil war-like case in the country.

I have been looking at ways to invest in water, EV charging stations, renewable energy investments and other things that would require sustainable investment in the future.

ESG fund

This is the new term where the analysts look at different companies and have very stringent criteria, wherein they look at three things, i.e., Environment, Social and Governance. The thinking of the fund managers has changed. They are looking at ESG investing, wherein many companies in various countries have started bringing Green Bonds as a form of investment. In India, we currently have ESG mutual funds. It was interesting to note that every fund manager has their own criteria for selecting companies.

Some of the criteria would be like the companies' future plan in renewable energy or cutting carbon emissions at a certain level or how much the company is contributing to air pollution and water pollution or what are the necessary steps they have taken for it, and whether the company is recycling the waste they have produced, and other similar factors keeping environment in mind.

As a retail investor, I would look at the listed companies who are involved in water treatment or waste management, such as ION Exchange – it is a water treatment company. What is the company doing regarding waste management and what kind of the waste they are producing, is that some kind of product which can be used in other stuff also?

Considering the social factor, an investor needs to look at whether the company is taking care of customer satisfaction or not. It is very easy to look at such companies as we keep on facing problems while using the products, how they are providing services to the customer, and whether there is any gender diversity or not. I have seen companies such as Shell petroleum and Hindustan Petroleum employ disabled people at their petrol pumps. So, all such factors can be seen while selecting companies. You might add additional criteria for selection, but it is undoubtedly your choice.

If I consider just India's scenario, the first thing I will look towards a company is who its promoters are and what their history is; not a detailed study is required, but some information regarding the promoters. How much the company is connected to political parties. I think this is a common scenario where companies take advantage to gain certain projects because of their good connections with political parties, even though I am not saying that all the companies do that, but certain companies do, and I know you might be aware which companies are doing such things.

Diamond Water Paradox

This was presented by Adam Smith, who observed the contradiction that, although water is more useful to humankind in terms of survival than diamonds, still diamonds command a higher price in the market.

Even though in India, it is challenging to invest in water, but there are various indexes in the world which allow you to invest in water, such as The Dow Jones U.S. Water Index, which is composed of approximately twenty-nine stocks, consisting of large companies that are affiliated with water business.

In India, a handful of companies are affiliated with water, such as Ion Exchange, Thermax, VA Tech Wabag and Triveni Engineering and Industries Ltd. I have been looking at the companies that are providing rainwater harvesting systems, but all of them are private companies that are doing good in their field. I have been also looking at investing in water since a long time. There is one more thing which we should know about – hydrogen. We have seen many companies bringing hydrogen powered cars, and even a bus was launched in India.

The Green, The Grey, The Blue

Before I move on and tell you about other things, let me first make you understand how the hydrogen economy is going to work and how I invested in few companies or have been betting on some.

I have been getting returns from investing in climate change and there are only a few companies which are listed on stock exchanges, and we can earn from them. Currently, Reliance is also entering renewable energy generation and there are companies like Suzlon which were already there in manufacturing, but have not performed very well, and even companies like Inox Wind Energy Limited.

Adani Green Energy Limited has been the strongest performer overall, and Adani Enterprises Limited, which owns a 100% share in Adani New Industries Ltd, is the second business I am keeping a watch on. The new energy business is into hydrogen and mainly green hydrogen. But rather than directly explaining how Adani will be benefitted, it is better to make you understand the overall hydrogen business.

Setting the table

Recently you might have seen in the news that, Nitin Gadkari inaugurated a hydrogen-powered bus made by KPIT-CSIR[5] and even Gadkari wants that we should have hydrogen power passenger vehicles in the market by 2030. In February 2022, the government launched a green hydrogen policy with the goal of producing five million tons of clean fuel per annum by 2030[6].

Looking at all these things, I wondered why even hydrogen is referred to in different colours.

- Grey Hydrogen
- Blue Hydrogen
- Green Hydrogen

Grey Hydrogen

Grey Hydrogen is derived and produced from natural gas, making it the least renewable form of energy. Currently, all of the hydrogen that India consumes is grey hydrogen. India consumes six million tons of hydrogen every year[7] and is producing through a process called steam-formation.

Unfortunately, almost 10 kg of carbon dioxide releases into the atmosphere for every 1 kg of grey hydrogen produced[8]. This high ratio of CO_2 generation gives this form of hydrogen

---

5 HT Auto Desk, 2022

6 Sudarshan Varadhan, 2022

7 Lou Del Bello, 2022

8 Jessica Shea Choksey, 2021

its grey designation. Looking at this ratio, it turns out that its impact is almost similar to drilling oil or mining. Here, the natural gas (we can say methane which is the primary element) is mixed with steam which yields carbon dioxide and hydrogen.

Blue Hydrogen

The same process or the same technique is used in blue hydrogen but the main difference is of handling of CO_2. With blue hydrogen, the CO_2 produced does not escape into the environment. Instead, it is captured at the production facility and stored separately. This technology is known as Carbon Capture and Storage (CCS).

Green Hydrogen

Here, electrolysis is used to separate the elements. Electricity is passed through water to separate hydrogen and oxygen. This process is costly as the electrolysis process uses electricity and if the electricity is produced from renewable sources such as wind, hydro or solar, then it is a loop wherein we are utilising and even producing green energy.

Reality check

Currently, due to war and a variety of other events occurring all over the world, such as floods, debt crises, and even drought and forest fires, that type of problem exists in the world. Not all countries have the per capita income of developed nations and installing solar, wind or even green hydrogen plants is costly.

The amount of space which all of them require and in

comparison to that, the energy generation goes to somewhere 25% for solar and 40-50% for wind. In comparison to the coal plant, the coal plant requires almost 1/3rd space and probably generate the same amount of electricity.

Forgetting what is happening all over the world, let us focus on India for the time being. The government also wants 24x7 electricity from renewable sources, for solar we understand that electricity is being generated from morning to evening 6 pm or 7 pm max, in summers. But what about the whole night? We still don't have enough wind farms installed in our country as compared to solar farms and we still have to think of fluctuation in monsoon and in winters.

For the rest of the time, the government is asking to have energy from hydrogen, especially green hydrogen, as we have started the adoption of electric vehicles in our day-to-day life. We would not like a condition such as California state where the electricity board had to request the consumers to not charge electric vehicles and not use electricity for some time to avoid blackouts[9].

This is how I have identified opportunities by looking at the current and future problems and the companies which are solving them.

ESG is the most oversold product

So how does one decide what shall be included and what shall not? Well, many use a negative screening approach to remove those particular sectors, such as coal mining and oil refining companies which are causing harm to the environment. But

9 Agence-France Presse | World News, 2022

then, how does ESG makes others give better returns. Or is it just the new term coined for the purpose of minting money by giving investors something new? Sometimes that is why I find, companies such as McKinsey, Deloitte, PwC and other consulting as well as investment banking firms – all they have done is come up with a new term which would mint them money.

Image Source: sustainabilityknowledgegroup.com

Let me give you some examples of what had happened when this particular term was not coined or was not over-sold.

During 1886, there was a company led by Jamsetji Tata which instituted pension fund and started giving accident coverage to their employees. In 1895, it became the first company to come up with 8-hour work day, installed fire humidifiers and sprinklers and gave additional benefits such as maternity leave, free medical aid, developed schools, profit sharing bonus and retirement gratuity. We all know that they are Tatas by the firm Tata Steel, and they pioneered ESG before the term was coined.

ITC[10], which derives the majority of its revenues from tobacco wherein such factors are negatively screened during selecting ESG companies, S&P came out with Index wherein from India, ITC is the only company to be included in the S&P ESG Index. The reason being ITC is the only company of its sheer size that is carbon positive (sequestering twice as much as carbon as it is emitting) and water positive also (harvesting four times more water than its net consumption for 30000 hectares of farmland in the process of irrigation).

Let me share with you my example as I am a businessman and I, a supplier of packaging material to Grasim Industries Ltd., Tata Chemicals Ltd. and Alkyl Amines Chemical Ltd. All of them are listed and I did not have to provide them any money to get into their vendor registration; it was all based on the quality of the material which I could provide to them and the capacity that I had. Nor do they accept corporate gifts because of their strict policies on governance. All I have to do is maintain a timely supply and I get paid on time.

So, do all companies do what they do because the millennials coined a term? Or it is in their nature to care about their employees and provide benefits to them. I know that Aditya Birla also provides similar benefits to their employees as Tatas do. In their early process of growing, the management understood that the company is what it is because of the hard work of employees, and they need to give them all those things back and create a good environment for society as a whole.

Now coming back to the marketers and bankers, they say that ESG provides better benefits, but there is no proof for

---

10 ITC, Sustainability

that, nor anyone has come up with any kind of number to support such arguments. Just because it is trending, many investors concerned about climate change and about the planet would be willing to accept low returns in the name of ESG. Many of them are doing this by keeping high expense ratio than other funds.What difference has it made when we are selecting good companies?

The companies which are performing well, have been doing good for their employees' benefit, for the society, for cost saving, for an increase in their profits, for reducing waste, and there wasn't a single reason for not doing so. Now the marketers are telling the companies that they would be able to have access to cheaper capital, but bankers being bankers still give cheaper capital to companies with good fundamentals, without caring whether the companies fall into ESG criteria or not. Listed companies, on the other hand, don't need to raise additional capital every now and then, considering few exceptions which are over leveraged. It is only the newer companies who are going to come with IPOs that might have a good story to sell.

What we might see over a period of time is that the companies might add some 50-60 pages to their annual report about boasting how good they are and how well they are keeping up with the requirements of ESG, and the marketers and bankers have shown the companies a way as in how to present themselves better to the audience that is listening to them. Because all the good companies have not boasted whether they are focusing on ESG, they know it from a long time, but bankers keep telling you for the sake of earning more. You should check the annual reports of Adani Green Energy Ltd., Reliance Industries Ltd., some other companies such as ITC and you will understand how many pages have been added to showcase the items which I just told you about.

These companies have to tell all these things and the CSR[11] which they do. You will soon understand the trend that all the companies have started focusing on that bit. Sooner or later, over the next 10-20 years, we are going to see some new terms coined up to keep investors intrigued.

Does ESG guarantee results?

While we all are investors; it is good to invest in ESG funds and all, but here comes the main question – does ESG funds guarantee results, or has it given better results than other funds which are not focused on ESG or compared to those fund managers which have been focusing on traditional companies? But the question which I have already raised is – how do I differentiate companies which should be considered in ESG funds or should not be considered in ESG funds?

Particulars	1 Yr Return	3 Yr CAGR Return	5 Yr CAGR Return	AUM (In Cr.)
SBI Magnum ESG Equity Fund	-0.72%	13.67%	12.28%	₹ 4,751.31
Axis ESG Equity Fund	-10.05%	6.42%	-	₹ 1,684.33
ICICI Prudential Equity Fund	-1.57%	10.19%	-	₹ 1352.91
Kotak ESG Opportunities Fund	1.44%	11.48%	-	₹ 1,305.40
Aditya Birla Sun Life ESG Fund	-11%	11.04%	-	₹ 962.83

Note: All funds except SBI Magnum ESG Equity Funds were launched in 2020, while SBI Magnum Fund was launched in 2013.

Data Source: Zerodha Coin[12]

11 Corporate Social Responsibility

12 I have added only these 5 funds because their AUM is above 800 Cr.

There is something interesting which I noted while gathering this data. There are few companies which are common in majority of these funds such as ICICI Bank, HDFC Bank, Infosys, Bajaj Finance, SBI, Axis Bank, TCS and Larsen & Toubro. While majority of the ESG funds gave negative returns over the last year, investing in Nifty 50 Index fund would have been better.

Particulars	1 Yr Return	3 Yr CAGR Return	5 Yr CAGR Return	AUM (In Cr.)
UTI Nifty 50 Index Fund	6.36%	14.87%	12.54%	₹ 9504.80
ICICI Prudential Nifty 50 Index Fund	6.31%	14.87%	12.42%	₹ 3,970.70
SBI Nifty Index Fund	6.35%	14.65%	12.32%	₹ 3,199.02

Data Source: Zerodha Coin

While comparing these funds, majority of the funds in the ESG criterial showcase lesser returns than low-cost Index funds mentioned above and even the Nifty 50 Index funds have all the common companies mentioned earlier.

The other remaining things

I have been looking at and understanding different things about climate change and the Paris Agreement to go to net zero in carbon emissions, and recently I have been reading the book called *How to avoid a climate disaster* and understood the implications of the human actions that are taking place. It is not simply important to invest in the proper businesses; it is also important to consider the cost of neglecting climate change.

Here in India, not many are concerned about climate change as the middle-class population is also recovering with the COVID 19 scenario, and the loss of life, as well as income has pushed many families back, and they have to start from scratch. Even though it might not be a concern for many as of now, it is impacting our lives and will continue to do so. This book is not just about investing in limited companies listed in NSE or BSE, but also about understanding that the world is currently facing a problem, and sustainable startups are required, which are not just going after growth but also sustaining themselves from revenues and growing organically.

Here it has become a trend nowadays to increase the valuation by showing how much the cash burn is to the investors, and how much is the growth potential. Investors won't mind investing in firms, why would they?

They are having exits after increasing the valuation, and even though we have some good companies such as BYJU'S, which are solving problems and, in this case, even Zomato, but is it worth investing in companies for a normal retail investor who is just making losses in the name of growth? Because the day funding stops, all these things start falling apart. I believe it is not the limited investment that is the reason for the losses of the company, but excessive cash and improper utilization of it in the name of growth is the reason of these valuation. Companies otherwise won't be having a scenario such as Oyo rooms, wherein they have started falling apart, and the one in Maharashtra also filed for bankruptcy.

I want to discuss the crypto mania and the buzz around it, but I have dedicated a whole chapter to it for a greater understanding of what is happening.

3.
How to spot great companies

Picking up winners is more an art than the science behind it. As Sherlock Holmes in the web series says, "*You see but do not observe.*" Now if you look at stocks, most people stop applying common sense and have a herd mentality while buying and selling. Just because it is easier to purchase and sell a stock, most retail investors keep selling when the stocks are going down. While most retail investors fall for the fool's theory which states that suppose investor A buys a stock at Rs 100, he expects some increase and then sell it at a certain price to investor B for a price of Rs 110. Now the, investor B expects the price to increase and sells it to investor C at price of Rs 130. This process continues until the stock becomes corrected because it was overvalued and the investors who have invested money while the prices were way high sell the stock at a loss.

Rather than selling the stock and looking at it as just a piece of paper or a number in your Demat account, start looking at it as a business because ultimately, you are going to invest in a business, and miracles don't happen in a year. They take time for at least 10-15 years to show the substantial difference and the growth it has achieved.

As in India, we consider McDonald's, a fast-food joint, as a delicacy. It is one of my favourite places to eat. So, if you owned a McDonald's which would be valued at one crore rupees, and after a few months somebody would ask to buy at ninety lakhs, you wouldn't sell it because the business is not doing well since last one month. If you would rather wait for higher valuation and then sell it when the business is performing at its best to get better returns, if at all you wish to exit from the business. Just because selling stocks is much easier than selling other assets such as real estate, it doesn't mean that you must sell it.

Liquidity preference for money

Though it is a concept of economics, it is very much useful while investing. We usually invest in companies to earn good returns and understand that this liquid asset can come to use, as and when required. Though it is better to understand the liquidity preference of money as investments are not made only in stocks, but also in real estate and gold as well as other commodities. It is interesting to know that when real estate sales and prices go up, investors' preference to invest in gold decreases. Most investors purchase gold as a hedge to their other investments. Gold and real estates have inverse relationship with each other.

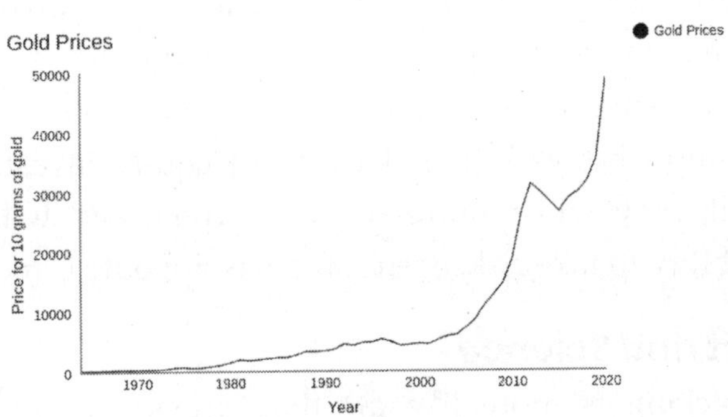

Source: Data Collected from Bank Bazaar

This graph presented shows immense growth in gold commodity prices, reaching Rs 5000 per gram. Over the years, we can also understand another thing as to why people invest in gold, the reason being that our currency or you can take any currency of the world, has lost its value when the gold standard was removed in the Bretton Woods Conference. Before the removal of Gold Standard, the value of the currency was derived from how much gold the Reserve Bank had in its vaults. It is also interesting to know all this was done because Federal Reserve didn't have enough gold in its vault to honour the cheques of the customers and thus we saw fractional reserve banking coming into mainstream.

People also invest in real estate as a means of earning capital gains. Whenever investors think that businesses are not doing well overall, or not having earnings according to the expectations, then they switch their investments either to gold or real estate as a means of getting better returns than the equity and bond market. Even though I am of the firm belief that over longer term period, it is better to invest in gold, equity and real estate, considering the age of the investor. If he is of eighty years or let's just assume more than sixty-five years, it is better to keep more portion of the wealth invested in long-term bonds rather than direct equity investments. After all, they will require regular income and will have lower ability to take risk, even if the risk appetite is more.

The Art and Science

Stock picking is more like art than science, as investors forget to use common sense. If you see, there are very few profitable franchises of pizzas in India which are listed on stock exchanges. There are many other master franchises, but many are privately owned companies. So, without any further thinking, if I just study its market share and invest in Jubilant Food Works, I would be earning a substantial amount without worrying about whether the company is functioning properly or not, because it can't function properly if it doesn't have a proper system in place. This does not mean that there won't be competition or private players won't be taking any market share. Jubilant Foods is just an example for you to understand because Domino's Pizza has pan India presence.

I like travelling a lot, and since I travel, new things come by experience, even though I travel mostly by buses and local transportations when visiting some new place. The journey tells a different story of the firm that is famous out there or is branding heavily and is the most accepted brand in a particular region. Now, if you are a college guy or even a father or mother, just google once and understand how many products Nestle India has in its portfolio. How many FMCG companies do you see when you are going to the mall and why again and again you keep on purchasing the same stuff you used to buy and don't even care to try new products.

I do not think that Maggi lovers would have tried taking Yippie noodles, Top Ramen, or other stuff available in the market. Most people don't even understand the differences in taste while drinking Coke and Pepsi. So just choose your favourite brand and know more about it and then decide whether it is wise to invest in that particular stock or not. Please don't do it because someone told you to purchase a stock, and then you don't even know what business they are into and how their industry works.

Even though many analysts use scientific approaches by using math and do quantitative analysis in their investment firm by creating complex models, but how do you tell someone who just made tenfold in Adani Green by investing early, or how do you say to a person who used to own MRF stock and made it huge without analysis, just by asking people and observing during the travel.

I believe that most would argue that this is not a great method to invest in companies, but how would I get convinced if I earn a minimum of 15-20% on the portfolio that I think are good businesses? Now I don't know whether you are into fitness or not, but I am just in love with Skechers because of the comfort they provide. It is not that I am suggesting a brand, but I have tried other brands also, but none of them is as good as this one. Don't you think I would be waiting for Skechers footwear to bring out an IPO in the Indian market and then invest in it?

Sometimes the tip works, and I don't know how and from where they have got that information, but, in my experience, the mysterious the source is, the more likely the information turns out to be true. One thing that Indians beat everyone around the globe is the people's networking. Just go to a paan shop, and you will understand why ITC has the highest market share. The most absurd answer I have heard on asking people who smoke that why don't they try other brands, and most of them have provided me with the same answer: *we don't get the same feeling*. If now I try to quantify the feeling, it would be a difficult and mostly impossible and futile exercise and then decide whether to buy ITC or not.

I almost forgot to mention the story about the tip thing in the stock market. I got a call from my uncle Keyur. Even though he is just a year older than me in relation, he is my uncle. He called me out of nowhere, and as soon as I picked up the phone, he asked me to buy Adani Enterprises. It is going to reach Rs 250 from Rs 220 within a month. I was like, but how can you be sure? The only response I received was, I got a tip and don't ask from where, but just do as I say.

I usually ignore such stuff and ignored what he said to me, but it turned out to be true that the stock gained more than Rs 250 and is currently trading at Rs 537. If I had listened to him at that time, I would have at least doubled my returns from the stock. This is the one time I remember getting a tip from close friends or relatives, but other times I do not remember. There was also a scenario when my friend invested in Vakranjee. To be true, I did not know what Vakranjee was doing in terms of business, so I never gave any suggestions at that time, but once he invested, he lost almost half his money by investing in just one share. I later learned when Tathagat came to me and said that he invested a major portion of his savings in Vakranjee and lost almost half. The reason why he invested was that it had the best technology at that time, but failed to understand that its promoters were not that good, and the stock had previously crashed because of some problem amongst the promoter group.

Who am I to judge whether the tip is good or not? It's just a gut feeling, and then I take a decision. Would you believe that I started to think about investing in climate change after a post I read on Instagram which said that after reading a research paper, Bill Gates suggested that investing in climate change would gain a return of more than 400% in the next twenty years. This is how I started researching and finding about investing in climate change.

Nifty 50 does not depict our GDP

Many of our retail investors believe that the Nifty, as well as Sensex, depicts our GDP performance and whether the country is growing or not. It is not the case anymore. For those who don't understand, Nifty is just an index created by National Stock Exchange wherein companies are given weights, and different companies in different industries are there. The index is just the number of how the sector might work and mostly the large caps that fulfil the criteria. Consider it as a sample and nothing more. Even in that, there are fifty companies wherein some are gainers, and some are losers. Majority of the time I have seen that it is because of a few handful companies that the index is moving ahead. The reason being that those handful companies are having more weightage as well as they are performing better than the rest of the peers which are there in the index.

You take any index in the world, you will find the same phenomenon happening because only a handful of the listed companies can deliver year on year performance and beat their own benchmarks. But even after some time, when the companies are very large, their growth is difficult to sustain.

4.
Cryptocurrency

While I am writing about cryptocurrencies, I have a firm belief that the technology on which all of the cryptocurrencies are based will definitely reduce the transaction cost and sooner or later, every country will come up with their own cryptocurrency. By the time I finish publishing the book there would be lots of volatility in the existing cryptocurrencies.

Who knows what the future might be? But I am pretty sure the governments won't allow decentralized currencies. While writing and researching, I have come to know that many don't understand what this is and how things work or how it will benefit society. Though I am a non-believer of the current cryptocurrencies formed by individuals who have become billionaires as well as millionaires by crypto gaining popularity.

Introduction to blockchain technology

Blockchain is a cryptographically secured ledger that tracks transactions on a decentralised ledger. Decentralised networks such as Bitcoin and Ethereum etc., are a collection of computers that works on consensus mechanisms - a set of rules of how data is shared and recorded amongst its network.

How does Blockchain works?

There are a few things that are critical components, that together make blockchain secure and make it work as it is now.

1. **Hash Function:** Hash functions are used to link one block to another and are key components in making it work. It has two important features. First, they compress a message or transaction or any kind of input into a value of a predetermined length which is known as the hash value. The hash value of the input is easy to calculate, but it is practically impossible to decipher the input message from the hash value. The second feature is that it is distinctive. For a given input, there is exactly one hash. So for the same input, the hash value remains the same, but if there is change even in a single character, the hash value changes.
2. **Public cryptographic key:** These cryptocurrency networks, such as Bitcoin and Ethereum or any other which you may be dealing in, used public and private keys to generate spending transactions and verify their validity. A private key is a value generated randomly by a digital wallet. It serves as a unique authorisation code or a password. A public key is like your account number, which is usually public and is linked mathematically through a private key.

   Every time you make a transaction, the wallet cryptographically signs using the private key. The network verifies the transaction using combinations of public and private keys. If they match, the network verifies the transaction and adds them to a block of the blockchain.
3. **Mining:** It is another essential feature that is critical. Mining is the process of validating blockchain

transactions. Participants who are mining are incentivised to earn crypto, as originally mentioned by Satoshi Nakamoto in his white paper, because it would require high computational power, time and electricity.

Intro to Cryptocurrency

It is nothing but something made up of ones and zeros in electronic format which has no value attached to it; while there are many lovers, there are people who don't believe in it. Let's start with the believers.

The idea behind Bitcoin was introduced in October 2008 after the financial crisis that collapsed and affected many countries all over the world. Bitcoin was developed by someone pseudo named Satoshi Nakamoto as a peer-to-peer electronic cash system by using Distributed Ledger Technology (DLT).

A distributed ledger is a type of database that may be shared amongst entities in a network. In this ledger, the entries are recorded, stored, and distributed across networks so that each participant has a matching copy of the digital database. One of the features of DLT is the usage of cryptography, which is an algorithmic process to encrypt the data, making it unusable if received by unauthorized parties. Thus, you know that Bitcoin requires verification of the transaction using this technology; if your transaction is not verified on the DLT, then the coins which you sold or transferred to someone else won't be received by another party and won't be usable for you also.

This was not a common problem, but many have faced these problems wherein their transactions were not verified and have lost the bitcoins from their account and don't know where they are as of now and lost the money which they paid to buy the bitcoins. This is near to personal experience as one of my friends lost money while doing such things when the Indian government said that it wouldn't be allowing companies to transact cryptocurrencies in India. If they still wish to do the transaction, the exchange platforms need to be registered outside the jurisdiction of India.

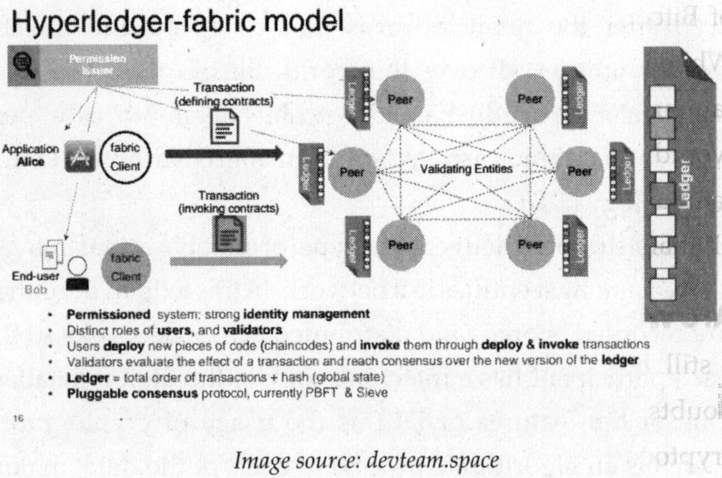

Image source: devteam.space

The above image explains how the whole thing works, which makes it almost hack proof.

Bitcoin uses blockchain technology which is a type of digital ledger in which information such as changes in the ownership is recorded sequentially within blocks that are then linked together using cryptography methods. Each block contains a grouping of transactions and a secure link to the previous block. Bitcoin's blockchain protocol requires all nodes to verify a new transaction and only then they are linked and added to a block. Since these computers are available and spread across the globe and run by various individuals, it is considered very difficult to hack them.

Unlike the reserve currency, which is USD or Swiss Francs or Euros, which the governments control as in the central banks which can print the money, Bitcoin has only 21 million coins that can be mined. There is a limited supply of Bitcoin, and it is estimated that it will run out by 2040. While I have talked about Bitcoin, it is because it is the most famous cryptocurrency as of now, and I don't know which would gain more publicity other than this. Ethereum is also a famous one, as well as Dogecoin, which was created as a joke, all thanks to Elon Musk, has gained too much popularity.

Are we sceptical?

I still have certain doubts, and even many legends have doubts about cryptocurrency's fundamental value. While the cryptocurrencies are created by the people and cherished by the people who do not have trust in the government and how they run the whole system, wherein the main purpose was to serve as a stable currency but has lost its sole purpose by being too volatile.

Let's understand why it has failed. There are three things that a currency for transacting must do and deliver:

1. It should be a unit of account, allowing one not just to value the assets and liabilities but also goods and services and also needs to be fungible in nature.
2. It should act as a medium of exchange which should be acceptable by buyers as well as sellers as a legal tender.
3. It should be able to store value, meaning that suppose you have Rs 100 with you, it will not lose the buying power – as in you will be able to buy something worth Rs 100.

Fiat currencies are nonetheless perfect, but they have had a long run and are in the system controlled by the Central banks of their respective countries, such as RBI, which controls the flow in India. Cryptocurrencies have seen extreme price volatility; it is not a bad characteristic as an asset, but a very bad one for a currency. I have seen investors broadly categorizing in three types of beliefs; the first is that they consider bitcoin as a form of collectibles, the second is they consider it as an asset compared to gold, and the third is they compare it to the reserve currency.

I can understand why investors consider it as a collectible as it is something new. The price is relative to the perception of the buyer, which any investor wants to give to it and compare to gold but something as a currency is unacceptable because of the volatility it has. Now let's assume you are a seller, and you deal in your favourite cryptocurrency. I am the buyer willing to purchase goods from you; let's say something as simple as a pizza. Suppose the price of one cryptocurrency is $50, and the pizza costs $50, so you won't be having a problem now, but because the cryptocurrency is very volatile, the value of one cryptocurrency is $65. So, I come to buy pizza when the value is $65 you are at a loss, but when I come when the value is less than $50, you are at a profit because the value of the cryptocurrency changes regularly. It loses the transaction value as a currency, and sooner or later, you will stop accepting cryptocurrency as a form of payment for your pizza, and I will have to pay cash whenever next time when I come to buy pizza.

Currently, the scenario is such that there are those who believe that it is nothing more than a Ponzi scheme or a pump and dump scheme, wherein large investors are earning money at the cost of small retail investors. As the markets are forward-looking, people have become very speculative regarding putting money in cryptocurrencies. I believe that if you wish to take the risk, you should invest some amount of your savings but not your life savings as many of them have done and gain short-term profit and have an exit from it.

Many investors understand that once all of these come under regulation, there won't be a money-making machine like this and will lose its speculative nature as it has now. Because many countries would be having their own cryptocurrency, and the acceptance of the current cryptocurrency, which is there in the market will be less. Even considering the long term, it is going to lose value. Let's say that the whole world starts accepting cryptocurrencies, then even though some are considered only limited in coins, there would always be the availability of alternatives in the market which can be used for transaction purposes. In the end, all it takes is nothing more than ten minutes to bring out new cryptocurrency. You must understand that the Ethereum does not have limitations on how many coins can be mined, which was created after Bitcoin. Now it is up to you to decide in what you consider the cryptocurrencies and how do you wish to utilize it.

There are various challenges that the DLT technology is facing now; as in when mining occurs, it uses a substantial amount of electricity because it requires a huge amount of solving complex problems as well as storing the data, which makes it less environment friendly. The regulatory approaches to this technology are different in different countries, and there is a lack of standardization. Also, there is a whole new mining industry set up in a few countries which I will be discussing in this chapter ahead.

Elon Cult

I have named this segment the Elon Cult because he has many followers, and because of that, he has been able to influence the demand for the cryptocurrency he likes, such as Bitcoin and Dogecoin. In his tweets, it is evident that he can manipulate or even joke about how the markets are moving. His Bitcoin announcement propelled him to new heights after he stated that he would start accepting Bitcoin as a payment for Tesla. It was at that similar point I came to understand that sooner or later, he is going to withdraw the statement because of the problems I stated above regarding the transactional nature of this currency, as well as conflicting with his own ideology regarding climate change and all his efforts of building Tesla going into vain.

It was in one of the early interviews he mentioned about the efforts of going to electric vehicles and combating climate change – that we all are in a ship that has a hole in it, and the water is coming in; all we can do is to slow the speed of water that is pouring in because of the hole.

As soon as he accepted Bitcoin as a payment for Tesla, its market value climbed to $830bn, near its peak.

Image Source: Twitter

His interest soon shifted to Dogecoin since it looked more entertaining to him, but more people began to speculate, so he eventually stopped just focusing on Bitcoin. It is not just Tesla accepting the payments but the whole supply chain of making a Tesla car, as well as the vendors supplying to Tesla, would have to accept Bitcoins to keep supplying to Tesla. A wider acceptance of Bitcoin would further fuel demand for

Bitcoins as fueling hopes that even other companies would start accepting other cryptocurrencies and would be able to serve large scale transactional value besides the reserve currency that we have.

It was after his U-Turn on accepting Bitcoins as payments for Tesla that many retail investors got furious and started a new coin called StopElon coin, which rose in price soon after it was created. It was just to show how furious the investors in the cryptocurrency were because of the random mood swings by Elon Musk.

I have seen the Elon effect taking place, and I assume that even you will be able to identify the effects from the three graphs which depict the price changes from one year and how the bitcoin has performed as well as Dogecoin because of his statements on Twitter as well as the statements made by him on behalf of Tesla accepting and rejecting the payments of Bitcoin.

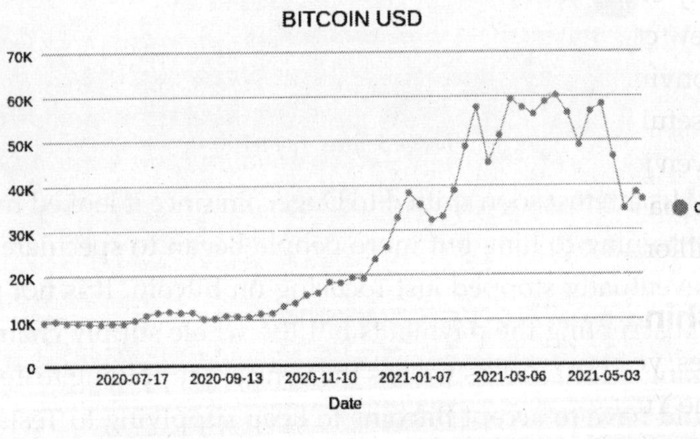

Source: Yahoo Finance

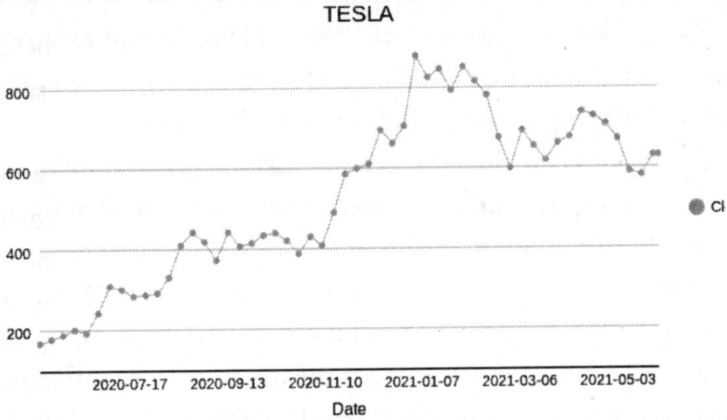

Source: Yahoo Finance

His moody Tweets have impacted even his share value of Tesla and his personal wealth, I would say. I don't know what the future will be for Bitcoin or Dogecoin, but I am certain to say that cryptocurrency will be the future and only just to have short-term trades to gain profit. I would invest in any of the cryptocurrencies, and what does it take to build a new cryptocurrency? Just ten minutes of time and very good convincing and marketing of the cryptocurrency and how useful it is, so that there is more demand for it. Sometimes I even joke with my friends to create a crypto with our names or based on our friendship; who knows? We might be a billionaire someday.

China's own cryptocurrency

Yes, you read that right. China has created a digital version of the Yuan and has started experimenting by circulating it with its citizens. While 1000 years ago, when the form of money was only coins; paper currency was created in China during the Song Dynasty during AD 960 – 1279. Promissory notes known as "Jiaozi" were printed by a group of merchants in Sichuan during the reign of Emperor Zhenzong[13].

We have seen that there is a constant power war going on between China and America, and China has been a step forward with creating a digital version of its currency. Even though there are already digital wallets such as WeChat in China, Paytm in India as well as PhonePay and Apple Pay in the USA, all of them are just means to move your money electronically. On the other hand, Yuan was created as a computer code which would function the same way as the other forms.

Other cryptocurrencies, such as Bitcoin, exist outside the traditional global financial system and aren't legal tender money like the cash issued by the governments. China's version of digital currency is controlled by its Central Bank, which would issue new electronic currency. As in the case of Bitcoin, it has anonymity for the user; here the Central Bank of China will be able to track the users as well as maintain the flow and would work on the principles of how currently the fiat money is utilized and not just the demand and supply of the currency.

In the recent months, more than one lakh people have downloaded a mobile phone app from the Central Bank enabling the citizens to spend small government handouts of the digital cash with merchants, including outlets of McDonalds and Starbucks. Beijing has even tested giving

---

13 James T.Areddy, 2021

cash with expiration which was a step to encourage users to spend money rather than save, which would, in turn, help the overall economy when the economy might need a jumpstart from a COVID -19 like scenario.

Now, this is not a currency made for speculation as it is being tightly monitored by the central bank and will have the same value without having differences in paper bills and coins. It is just like the central bank printing money or increasing circulation but only when required. The central bank will control the whole thing, and thus, there won't be any volatility associated with it to speculate. Unlike electronic transactions taking place today, the digital Yuan is designed to move from A to B instantaneously, even faster than what IMPS takes time, removing the need for banks and financial apps that are currently in the market. The only middleman remaining would be the central bank, reducing the transaction cost as mentioned earlier in this chapter.

The final legislation has not yet been made by China regarding the digital currency, but sooner or later, there will be many countries bringing their own digital currency by looking at China's example. While reading many articles about cryptocurrency, I found that more than sixty countries are at some stage of studying or developing their own digital currency, which would definitely reduce the value of current cryptocurrencies in the market.

I recently learned that the Bahamas has already issued digital currency to address financially underserved citizens and is controlled by its central bank. Currently, the electronic payment transfer takes days while doing international fund transfers with digital currency, wherein the intermediary is the central bank, could happen within a few minutes or seconds might happen that the Yuan would be more preferred as a form of digital currency if other countries don't have their own digital currency.

If all these become successful and the countries come out with their own digital currency, there are chances that physical cash and coins in circulation would be very less by saving a great amount of resources currently being utilized, and at that time, those resources could be used for some other purpose.

Investing with a bit of safety

A cryptocurrency should solve a problem in real life and make our lives easier; otherwise, there is nothing there in it for investing. During the interview which I took to understand investing in the technology with an expert, I realised that it is similar to analysing a stock which is listed on exchange platforms, and there is a definite need to remove the weeds from the grass, and that is why there are many useless cryptos in the market which are good for the short term if you want to do gambling. As I don't gamble, I made the decision to learn more from the professional. As a result, I am now certain that I understand how to make long-term investments in the cryptocurrency market in the event that I ever decide to start investing in cryptocurrencies.

The concept of ROHAS was very well explained in the interview:-

R - Revenue (How the coin earns revenue or the platform earns revenue). Read Whitepapers!

O - Organisation (What type of organisation it is, who are the founders?)

H - History of the organisation and the founders and any other detail which you wish to look for.

A - Algorithm (What type of algorithm is there in place). So you don't make a blunder by investing in the wrong coins.

S - Source code (How are they solving bugs? How many developers are working and updating the code?)

Frankly speaking, I am a non-technical guy and won't understand the A & S of ROHAS. Still, anyone can understand other things and the story which is written in whitepapers. If we do this much research, the last two points of ROHAS can be understood by someone who understands all these algorithms.

But, reading whitepapers would make the task easier as it would enable us to ask the right questions to the consultant or the developer and would enable us to prevent huge losses in future.

5.
IPO Frenzy

We all go crazy when we hear about IPOs that companies bring in order to raise funds. Many retail investors invest only to benefit from the extensive trading that happens in the expectation that they will benefit from the IPOs opening at a premium price and they will have a listing gain from it.

Soon after having a capital gain, even though it is for a short term, they exit, many investors do it this way, and when the stock goes up or down, they don't think as to why it has happened.

There have been 391[14] IPOs from 2017-2022[15], wherein almost 70% of the IPOs made the investors' money through listing gains.

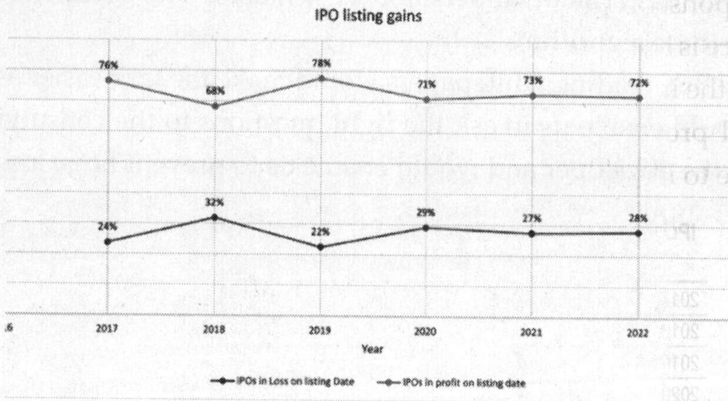

Image Source: Data collected from BSE

---

14 IPO Performance Tracker, 2022

15 It is till the month of Aug 2022

If we look at the year 2021, there have been ninety-one companies which have raised funds through IPOs. It is not that the IPOs are always successful after a year or a few years after investing in the stock. There have been many cases which I know, and one of the cases which I remember is when I was pursuing my master's where the IPO was oversubscribed a lot.

Suppose you know Astron paper & Board Mill Ltd., which was oversubscribed 242.72 times. I don't know what investors saw in that IPO that it was oversubscribed so much. The company is one of my friend's relatives', and fortunately, there were a few friends in the same business of manufacturing the Kraft paper who explained to me what all goes behind and what is the scope and margins.

The IPO debuted at a 130% premium over the issue price. It got listed on NSE at Rs 115 as against the issue price of Rs.50 per share. The Rs 70 Crore IPO garnered an amazing response in 2017, and then, in the current scenario, the share price is below the issue price, resulting in diminishing returns for the investors, with the current market price being Rs 37.50 and proving it to be a failed company which has not been able to increase the shareholders' wealth.

IPO Year	IPOs in Loss WRT Listing Date	IPOs in Profit WRT Listing Date	% in Loss
2017	20	68	22%
2018	24	67	27%
2019	12	37	24%
2020	7	24	23%
2021	23	68	25%
2022	8	35	19%
		Mean	23%

Source: Data collected from BSE

Similar to the example mentioned above, there have been many IPOs which have not provided results after being listed on the exchanges, such as Quick Heal Technologies Ltd., which was issued at Rs 321 and is now trading at Rs 208. There is IRFC which is a PSU that was listed at Rs 26 and is now trading at Rs 20.6 per share. There are many examples which can be given about the IPOs which have failed to perform after many years of being listed on the exchange platform and many IPOs which have debuted at a discount, such as the famous IPO of LIC, which have not performed even though it is a popular brand name amongst the Indian consumers and have the highest market share amongst the peers.

Even though many have failed to understand that there were some serious concerns regarding the IPOs, which resulted in LIC being called a failed IPO. So, to understand better about how to invest in IPOs, let us dwell in the history and how it became famous.

Diving into History

The first IPO ever to be noted down in history was made by the Dutch East India Company in August 1602. According to historians, this IPO made a difference as the company invited every Dutchman to invest in the company to help finance its trade in spices and other commodities. This made a huge difference than all other IPOs preceding this company's IPO, which was that earlier, the companies asked for a sum of money from a small pool of private investors and not the general public as an open invitation to all those who wished to invest.

The company's first charter was granted for twenty-one years. The company existed for a very long time – more than two centuries, but looking at its predecessors, which was a time period of 3-4 years only, twenty-one years was quite a long period of time. The company authors would have realized that it was quite a long time, and the investors might lose interest in subscribing to the IPOs.

While drafting the papers, they included a chapter that allows the investors to sell the shares they hold to other investors who are willing to purchase them. This provision meant that the investors didn't have to wait for ten years while the statements and general ledger or balance sheet were prepared for the first time.

In the USA, IPOs date back to the 1700s wherein the Bank of United States brought in its IPO. If we talk about India, Reliance issued the first IPO on stock exchanges even before SEBI was formed, becoming the first Indian company to issue its IPO. Technically even though it was the Dutch East India company, they were the first British company to do so.

In the centuries that followed, many great companies came up with their IPOs and the investors invested in them, such as MRF, Bajaj Finance, Bank of Baroda, and many more which you know of.

Why do companies come up with IPOs?

We all know that companies have been working efficiently, and the majority of them are privately owned, so when the companies need further money in order to expand the business, they go for IPOs as it is cheaper in comparison to going to venture capital or a bank loan.

While in IPOs, the company doesn't have to pay any interest to the shareholders of the company, only the dividends and that too not annually. You might have seen companies like Berkshire Hathaway don't pay dividends to their shareholder, but rather, the shareholders benefit from the capital appreciation of the share because of the company's performance.

In addition to just raising funds for expansion, companies also bring out issues in order to pay down their debts, which they have had either from banks or different investors and also reduce the interest cost which they might be bearing while paying back.

Another benefit of becoming a publicly traded company is that the company gets the benefit and attention in the eyes of the public and gains gravitas, and can even have better terms from their creditors and vendors.

As an investor, it is also important to look at why the company is raising funds. Is it raising just so that the promoters can earn money? In the case of LIC, it was just so that the government could reduce their stake in order to raise money from the investors to reduce the deficit the government was facing during that time. You might have seen that there are things such as Offer for Sale and Fresh Issue of Equity.

In an offer for sale, the existing shareholders or the promoters are diluting their stake. They are getting the money for themselves, as I mentioned above, the case for LIC investors. Still, in a fresh issue of equity, the investors are getting new equity wherein the capital has been increased for the company in order to raise money. While reading the

DRHP[16] that is the draft red herring prospectus that the company needs to submit, it always mentions the number of shares which are given for the fresh issue of equity and the number of shares that are there for an offer for sale.

So, these are the primary reasons which I mentioned to you as to why a company comes up with their IPOs, and now you know that it is mostly to raise funds for either capital expansion, reducing their debts and moving forward, or to gain more access to different kinds of market mechanisms.

Things to consider for applying for the IPOs

Usually, I don't apply for IPOs anymore because it is the seller's market, meaning that companies spend a hefty amount and investment bankers do their job while giving them media coverage and other coverage which is needed in order to make it a successful IPO, as even the investment bankers' fees are dependent on the IPO.

We all are eager to look into IPOs because of the listing gain; because why not? If my money gets doubled or even rises 20-25% in a day, which other genuine method of investing will give me such better returns? If I take an average retail investor, investing Rs 15000 is also a huge amount, and the majority of the retail investors don't have the luxury of keeping their investments for a longer time horizon of even 3-4 years in equities.

- The first thing that needs to be considered is that you need to open up the DRHP, which is available online and is free of cost. Look for the auditor's report and read

16 Draft Red Herring Prospectus

what the auditor mentioned regarding the company. I can guarantee that the auditor is not going to state anything wrong because his reputation and work is going to be on the line.

- The second point would be to understand the market and know why the company is raising money and how do they intend to gain from the investment.
- The third is to look into the cash flow statements of the company and try to understand how the company has performed, whether the company is earning its operating income more than it is investing, or if there are constant fluctuations in the operating revenue. As well as reducing the capital expenditure, if any it has done so far, is it able to generate free cash flow i.e., if you subtract capital expenditure from operating income, the number should be above zero.[17]
- The fourth point is to look at the directors of the company and must have a background check, you can just google, and you will find out how the directors are, whether any of the directors have fraud charges or not, and whether the composition of directors is family or relatives. When you look for them and find out that the majority of the board is comprised of relatives, then this can be considered as a red flag, as it is being managed by the CEO only, and the rest or majority of the board

17 Sometimes even good companies that have been giving returns on consistent basis have negative free cashflows to the firm, but that is usually once in 6-7 years when they are investing considering the demand.

members are just puppets for the CEO.

Suppose you happen to find any of the red flags mentioned above or even look into the company while applying for IPOs. In that case, there are chances that you won't lose money if the analysis is done in the said manner. You might also find companies wherein the coverage is not given to them, or very less amount of coverage is given to a company. The reason being that promoter doesn't need to spend a hefty amount in order for the investors to give them confidence so that they invest in the company.

In the year 2022, there have been new age tech companies which applied for IPOs, and investors lost their wealth. For example, if you had invested in Paytm IPO which was publicized way too much, the share price slipped 27% on the day of the listing and investors lost nearly Rs 2835 crores[18]. On the other hand, Adani Wilmar has managed to perform and give better returns to the investors.

If you had remained invested in FSN E-Commerce which is the Nykaa company, you would have had 36%[19] negative returns because of the downfall in the share price. There are many examples, and the list goes on and on, so it is better to follow the four things which are mentioned above and then only invest in an IPO.

Paytm Fiasco

I would like to talk about this company because it was one of the first companies whose share price tanked 27% on the

18 Rukhaiyar, 2021

19 This is considering that you might have invested in it during its IPO and remained invested till now. Dt: 06/08/2022

listing day. I have written an article on LinkedIn[20] on the Paytm Fiasco and why it failed to give returns on the listing day.

Paytm shares tanked on the listing date, probably because its founder, Vijay Shekhar Sharma, failed to mention how the company would be profitable in the near future or in the coming years. In his speech, he did mention that the company is going to enter into new segments in order to deliver more products to the customers, but entering into new segments and gaining market share is a completely different ball game, which Paytm has not been able to deliver to the shareholders.

Paytm and similar other startups have kept the focus in burning cash in order to gain market share and have taken the Hockey Stick Approach[21], and have failed to deliver on promises.

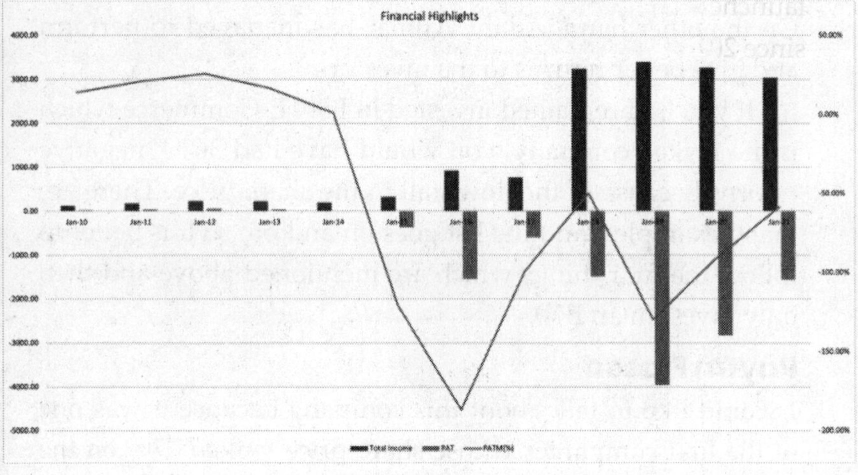

Source: Ace Equity, Own Research

---

20 Brahmbhatt, 2022

21 Explained in the different chapter

Looking at the company's financial highlights, it has not been profitable for a long time. If we consider any traditional business, the main focus of that business will be growth and profitability without compromising any of the things.

If we look a few years back, then you would remember that there was demonetization done by the government wherein there was a cash crunch for a few months. But even looking at that, Paytm failed to capture a substantial market share. One thing I find astonishing is that it should have had more revenue after covid lockdown, but if you look at 2021 data, it seems that the revenues started declining, which brings the possibility that it is losing market share to its competitors.

Paytm, which is the leader in the wallet segment, is losing its market share in other segments because the government launched UPI, and the growth of UPI has been tremendous since 2016.

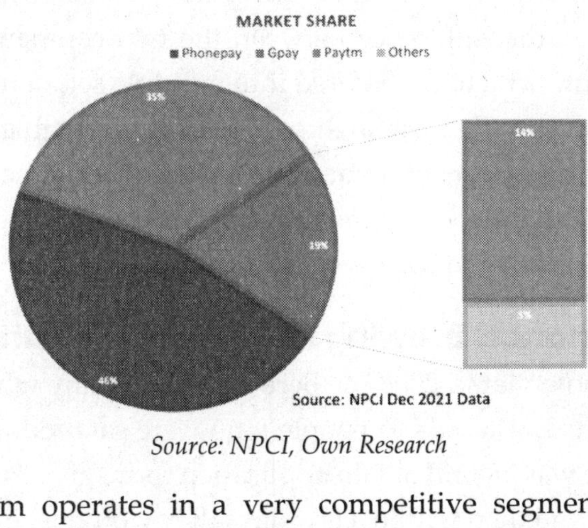

Source: NPCI, Own Research

Paytm operates in a very competitive segment in the industry wherein it has failed to leverage the situation as of now in its favour, but, as it is growing its lending business, it might be able to capture a slice in the lending business. If we look at the e-commerce space, Amazon and Flipkart are the market leaders; in the insurance segment, if we look into private players, there are well-established players such as HDFC Life Insurance, ICICI Lombard General Insurance, Bajaj Finserv and many other players. Even in ticket bookings, there is BookMyShow; and the lending space, there are many NBFCs such as Bajaj Finance, HDFC, etc.

All these things are okay, considering it provides shareholders with some type of value either in capital gains or in the form of dividends. But it needs to be profitable, otherwise there won't be too much justification for the share price that the investors are paying.

Now let me give you an example of Bajaj Finance which is one of the peers and understand how it has grown. You will realize the difference between the two companies that how Paytm, which has entered into multiple segments is not able to have market leadership or become profitable and on the other hand, Bajaj Finance has focused on financing and entering into different segments and has remained profitable as well as been able to reduce their cost.

Bajaj Finance: brewing financialisation ahead

We all know that in 2008-09 there was a company which was offering its EMI cards to people who were salaried. All they had to do was just fill out an application form, give their PAN numbers and then within a few days they would receive their cards which were similar to debit and credit cards. But the difference about this was that it used to give EMI facility on more than fifty different categories of products that were not available earlier.

Product suite **BAJAJ FINANCE LIMITED**

Consumer	SME	Commercial	Rural	Deposits	Payments	Partnerships & Services
BAJAJ FINANCE LIMITED						
1. Consumer Durable Loans 2. Digital Product Loans [E] 3. Lifestyle Product Loans 4. Lifecare financing 5. EMI Cards 6. Retail spend financing 7. 2-Wheeler & 3-Wheeler loans 8. Personal Loan Cross-Sell 9. Salaried Personal Loans [E] 10. E-Commerce financing 11. Retailer finance 12. Health EMI Card	1. Unsecured Working Capital Loans [E] 2. Loans to self employed and Professionals [E] 3. Secured Enterprise Loans 4. Used-car financing 5. Medical equipment financing	1. Loan against securities 2. IPO financing 3. ESOP financing 4. Vendor financing to auto component manufacturers 5. Financial Institutions Lending 6. Light Engineering Lending 7. Specialty Chemicals Lending	1. Consumer Durable Loans 2. Digital Product Loans 3. Lifestyle Product Loans 4. Personal Loans Cross Sell 5. Salaried Personal Loans 6. Gold Loans 7. Loans to Professionals	1. Retail Term Deposits 2. Corporate Term Deposits 3. Systematic Deposit Plan	Issuance 1. PPI 2. UPI 3. BBPS Acquiring 1. Merchant QR	1. Life Insurance Distribution 2. General Insurance Distribution 3. Health Insurance Distribution 4. Pocket Insurance [#] 5. RBL Co-Branded Credit Card 6. DBS Co-Branded Credit Card 7. Financial Fitness Report
BAJAJ HOUSING FINANCE LIMITED						
1. Salaried Home Loans [E] 2. Salaried Loan Against Property 3. Affordable housing finance	1. Loan Against Property 2. Self Employed Home Loans 3. Lease Rental Discounting	1. Developer Finance 2. Commercial Construction Finance 3. Corporate Lease Rental Discounting	1. Loan Against Property 2. Home Loans 3. Secured Enterprise Loans			
BAJAJ FINANCIAL SECURITIES LIMITED						
1. Trading Account [E] 2. Depository Services [E] 3. Margin Trading Financing [E]	4. HNI Broking 5. Retail Broking [E] 6. IPOs and OFS	7. Mutual Funds [E] 8. Distribution of PMS 9. Proprietary Trading				

(E) Also available through digital channels 22

Image Source: Bajaj Finance Annual Report

Over the years it has managed to grow from more than fifty categories to the above-mentioned product suite in the image. It now has two more subsidiaries with 100% holding in them which is Bajaj Housing Finance Limited which is focusing on home loans, specifically talking about affordable housing loans as well as giving finance to builders who construct these houses or apartments. In financial securities, it has done good with similar lines such as ICICI securities or even Zerodha and is providing similar services to the consumers.

I believe both these companies will grow, the reason being the financialization of the economy as we have adopted UPI and are doing ten trillion transactions as well. The new generation is having confidence in financial markets and are willing to take risks by investing in the markets. Even the ratio of financial savings to total household savings is increasing and millennials are buying more financial products rather than physical products such as homes and gold.

Strong distribution reach **BAJAJ FINANCE LIMITED**

Active distribution	30 Jun 2019	30 Jun 2020	30 Jun 2021	31 Dec 2021	31 Mar 2022	30 Jun 2022
Consumer durable stores - Urban	22,000+	24,200+	26,900+	29,500+	30,600+	31,000+
Consumer durable stores - Rural	15,200+	19,600+	24,000+	27,900+	29,800+	31,500+
Digital product stores	23,100+	26,400+	26,350+	28,800+	29,500+	31,150+
Lifestyle retail stores	8,300+	9,500+	9,400+	10,800+	11,000+	11,050+
EMI card - retail spends stores	20,700+	24,300+	14,500+	17,800+	18,800+	20,050+
Bajaj Auto dealers, sub-dealers & ASSC	4,900+	5,500+	5,800+	6,000+	6,000+	5,550+
Non-captive 2W dealers, sub-dealers & ASSC*	-	-	-	-	-	1,170+
DSA/Independent Financial Agents	2,800+	4,900+	7,500+	7,500+	7,500+	7,500+
Overall active distribution network	97,000+	1,14,400+	1,14,400+	1,28,300+	1,33,200+	1,38,900+

Image Source: Bajaj Finance Annual Report

In recent few years from Covid-19 till now, the company has been able to grow more than 41000 distribution points which would enable more customers to opt for those cards and use the facility provided by Bajaj Finance.

While doing all these things, it has now a customer franchise of 60.3 million customers who are using the app or the cards on regular basis as well as out of those almost 30mn customers have access to two-wheeler loans which is one of the new categories it has entered into.

Setting the table

In this section, I would be covering the key points which have grown over the years and have helped Bajaj Finance to grow.

- It has made strategic tie-ups with Cars 24, DBS bank and RBL bank. As the market for second-hand cars is going up since Covid, it has become beneficial for the company as well as the banks. It has started providing co-branded credit cards to expand its horizon which would benefit the companies as well as the banks.
- It has QR deployment at 18000 branches or touch points and is expanding it to one lakh touch points which would enable them to capture even more data on the payments. In the longer run, the company would be able to lower the cost of funds from what it is now.
- The company is adding digital EMI cards, as in you don't need physical cards which we usually have in wallets. This would even lower the cost of the company in distribution as well as in developing physical cards. With the enablement of 5G, I think this would be extremely beneficial to the company as currently, they have 70000 customers who have digital cards. I don't know whether you understand this concept or not, but even Bank of Baroda is providing digital debit cards which can be used at every place except on a POS machine as of now. Soon we might not require physical cards on the POS machine also.
- It also has 155 standalone gold loan branches wherein it is competing with Muthoot Finance and are planning to increase the branches to 232. Even though all these things are mentioned, it has its geographical presence in 3700 locations all over India, except Jammu and Kashmir.
- Over the years, it has been able to reduce the cost of

funds with the current cost of funds being 6.64% or you can also understand it as the cost of capital. It is higher than banks as it is NBFC but still, this company has an impressive track record.

Financials

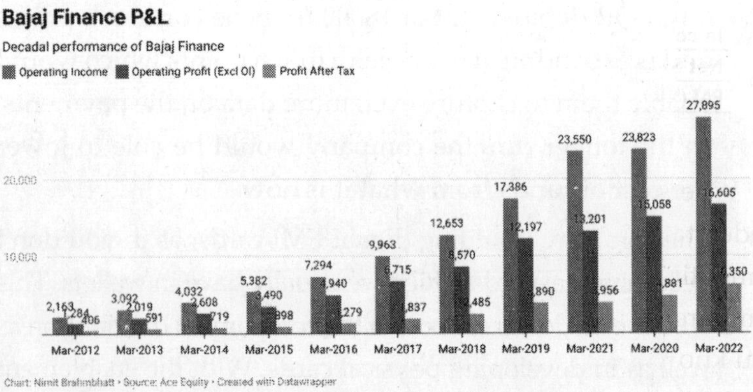

Data Source: Ace Equity, Own research

Looking at the picture you would understand that it has been able to grow at a fast rate and slowed down only after Covid-19 wherein again it has been able to improve its performance.

Bajaj Finance	**Growth in CAGR**			
Particulars	**1 year**	**3 years**	**7 years**	**10 years**
Revenues	18.45%	17.07%	26.50%	29.14%
Operating Profit (Excl. OI)	25.78%	10.83%	24.96%	29.18%
FCFF	60.55%	17.74%	32.24%	31.64%
Share Price	40.98%	33.88%	50.78%	57.11%
Adjusted EPS	60.10%	16.00%	28.74%	27.12%

Note: CFO is not calculated for Bajaj Finance as the concept of CFO is not applicable to financial companies. As well as in FCFF, PAT is used in calculating the growth of the compounding.

Data Source: Own Research, Ace Equity

When you see the image above, you will realize the company's growth over years. 1-year performance and the remaining years so that you as an investor can decide, what is your ideal time period of investment and whether the company is able to perform or meet your return expectations or not.

In comparison to Industry	FY 22	FY 21	FY 20
Net Sales (%)	**17.16**	**9.9**	**10.5**
PAT (%)	21.14	21.19	20.15

Data Source: Own Research, Ace Equity

When you compare it with the industry you will further understand that it was able to capture the market from its competitors. In 2020 it represented 10.5% of net sales when compared it with the industry, but when you look at FY 22, you know that it now comprises of 17.16% of the industry in terms of doing net sales. Even in terms of profits, it has been able to jump from 20.15% to 21.14%, meaning that the cost of customer acquisition is not very high as compared to new age fintech companies.

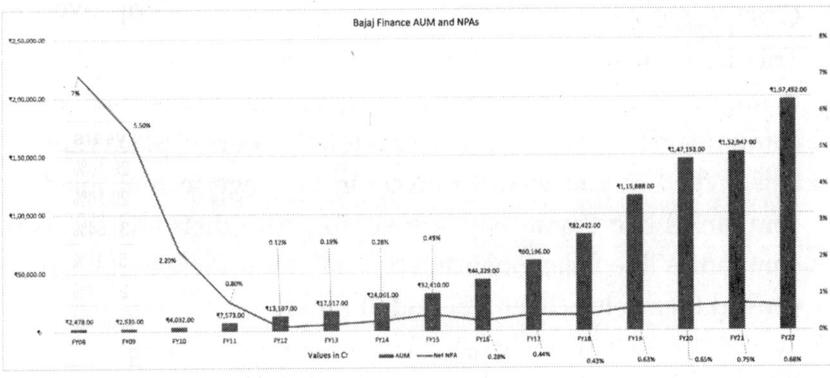

Data Source: Own Research, Ace Equity

When it is a financial company, we also think about whether it has been able to maintain its NPAs or not.

In 2008 it had NPAs of 7% and this was just about the time we entered into a financial crisis wherein there was Lehman Crisis. Because of the availability of information of PAN cards, it was easy for the company to get credit scores or develop its own scoring mechanism and reduce NPAs.

Further, it was able to beat its competitors in a way that there would be companies who would charge fewer interest rates, thus consumers with low credit scores and less credit availability would shift to their competitors wherein the competitor would acquire consumers whose chances of defaulting were higher. The other companies cannot charge higher than Bajaj Finance and companies on similar grounds would have to spend heavily to acquire new customers which in turn would reduce their PAT and ROE. Thus, Bajaj Finance benefited from all these and became a big data company which is now focusing on customers with better accuracy than its competitors.

Conclusion

This is my take on Bajaj Finance, you might also feel that it might be biased or may believe in the story I told in comparison to Paytm – the choice is totally yours to place your bets. Whether you want to invest in new age tech enabled companies like Paytm who are yet to prove their mettle, or companies like Bajaj Finance who have been there and have proved themselves over a period of time.

From Nithin Kamath

Recently Nithin Kamath, the CEO of Zerodha, posted on LinkedIn[22] that every time the favourite retail stock of the investors, which has been given way too much coverage, falls, the number of investors who buy those stocks goes up in order to reduce their average buy price, thinking that it might go up in future or the company is kind of a turnaround where the investors might benefit in the long term with an example shared of Zomato.

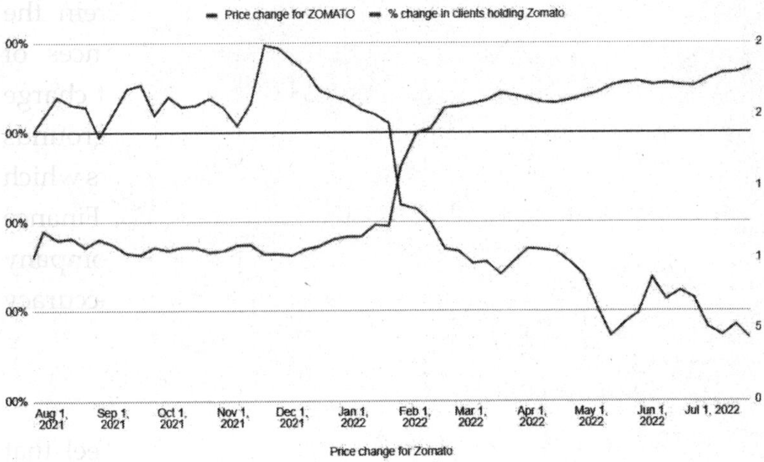

Image Source: Nithin Kamath LinkedIn

All this brings further clarity that it is not good to invest in bad companies or IPOs, and we need to sell the losers of our portfolio and buy good companies. It can be clearly seen that investors have lost a great amount of money while sticking to the company after IPO even though the IPO was

22 Kamath, 2022

successful but failed to deliver substantial results according to the shareholders' expectations.

You all must be thinking why I am mentioning Zomato and Paytm over and over again; it is because these are the new age companies who have used technology in the best possible manner but failed to create a good business model. Another reason is that during its IPO, many retail investors were buying the shares because they have the familiarity with the company because of daily usage, but no knowledge regarding the business model and functioning of it.

6.
Understanding the market structure

We frequently make investments in industries that we don't fully understand. When the market declines, we worry, and when we lose money, we point the finger at others rather than trying to figure out why a certain industry or market segment is acting in a certain way. Is it because of the FIIs that are taking the money back, or there are some fundamental changes in the business, or else your business is into a sector which is affected by the government economic reforms, policy changes or because of the reserve bank decisions that might impact the business that you have invested in.

Now that majority of the people have the same problem. Let us understand the different markets in which companies work, and it might help you to make better decisions while investing in them.

Monopoly

Monopoly businesses are the types of business in which there is an absolute monopoly, and no other companies are making the product, except you. Companies in pharma or tech companies might have such an edge, because of the patent which the company has, which gives the company the advantage of manufacturing it solely and the other companies are not allowed to copy it and reproduce the thing without the permission of the person/company who has the rights.

There are different kinds of monopoly, which varies according to area, such as Tata Power Ltd., Mahanagar Gas Ltd., Vadodara Gas Ltd., Reliance Power Ltd., Power Grid Corporation of India, Adani Total Gas Ltd. and many more companies, which are into such sectors, because if you look at all these companies, they have a monopoly in the market, the place where they are doing business.

Now imagine a scenario where there are two power distribution companies which are doing business in the same city. It would be very difficult to generate profits and won't be a sustainable business as the investment is very large, creating a monopoly in itself. Similarly, businesses like ports create a monopoly in the area. Let's say you have some business at Mundra Port; you will have to go to Adani as it is handling the port. No person or another company can develop a port besides a port without making heavy Capex and understanding the profitability portion of running the port.

It would never be, that one day someone will come and start a port besides Adani Ports, thus creating a monopoly situation for the business, as well as the people who are using the port have to accept the services which the particular port provides as well as the rate at which it offers because you don't have an option. The only option someone else has is to go to a different port, which might increase the transportation and handling charges for the business.

These are the businesses which have a monopoly because of the location advantage they have, but it is not that we only have one port in India. The second type of monopoly is of the product monopoly; wherein there is a patent or the companies which have a kind of monopoly based on the market share they hold in the market of their particular product. Or maybe because of the government regulations which none other companies are allowed. Companies such as IRCTC hold a 100% market share in ticket bookings. Even though you might be thinking that there are other platforms through which you can book tickets, such as Paytm, MMT, PhonePe and others, all of them are connected with IRCTC, wherein without your account in IRCTC, you won't be able to book a ticket, or else you will have to go to an agent who does it on your behalf.

Then there is Nestle, which manufactures the brand Cerelac, the instant cereal which is used for infants of six months and even has various ranges which go till the child reaches the age of 3-4 years. It has a market share of 97%. There are chances you won't find an alternate product in your nearby store because every infant product is stacked with Cerelac.

Even there are companies which you know or use on a regular basis such as Parachute Oil and Saffola, which are the brands of Marico which has 70-75% market share in edible oil and then the Parachute Oil which holds a market share of around 50-55%.

The last company which I would like to write about is ITC. You all know ITC, which holds almost 75-80% of the market share in cigarettes because of the distribution channel it has developed and the economies of scale it generates.

There are many examples, but as an investor, while

looking at the businesses, we must understand how to look into the markets and which type of businesses to invest in.

If you are a rational investor who wishes to go safe, then the companies as mentioned earlier are worth investing in. Still, suppose you wish to take on some risk; in that case, you should avoid companies which have only locational advantage but rather look for companies such as Nestle, Marico and Pidilite, which have the product advantage and are beating the competition because of the quality of the product, the distribution of the product and their ability to pass on any cost increment which they face due to inflation to the end consumers.

I would recommend avoiding government-owned companies because the government might take a certain decision which might hurt the investor sentiment and even hurt the ROCE of the companies.

You might remember the incident[23] wherein the government came up with the decision to take off 50% share from the convenience fees that IRCTC earns, which resulted in bad investor sentiment and resulted into a downfall of the share price, and the government had to take back the decision because of all the things that happened to the share price.

Another case happened in the banking sector; Yes Bank was on the verge of bankruptcy because of the Rana Kapoor scam, and consumers were not willing to keep their savings in Yes Bank. As it was such a large bank which might result in large unemployment and a chain reaction causing the 2008 financial crisis scenario as to what happened to the Lehman

23 Chiranjivi Chakraborty, 2021

Brothers, the government intervened by directing SBI to infuse capital into Yes Bank and become one of the largest shareholders of Yes Bank[24]. This led to SBI investing in the funds to save Yes Bank rather than elsewhere, which would have generated more returns and better ROCE. On the same day, the shares of SBI decreased by 3%.

Monopolistic

This is a type of market where there are few sellers and a large number of buyers. Here the demand for the product is similar as well as the type of the product that is being offered is almost the same, but companies are selling into different segments.

This type of market structure can be seen for groceries that we buy, the garments required for day-to-day activities, cosmetics and even medicines such as Dolo 650 or Crocin pain relief. There are even other companies which are there in this market.

Let me explain you the garment market. If you look around, you will find only a handful of companies which are there in the market which provide garments to the Indian consumers.

Page Industries, a manufacturer of undergarments primarily and other casual clothes are offering its product to premium customers or consumers who can pay a certain price. Similarly, on the other hand, there is Rupa selling *aaram ka maamla,* Dixcy Scott, VIP, Dollar and other brands which are there in the market have substantial market share. Even though they are offering similar products, each of them

24 Govt asks SBI to form consurtium to buy stake in Yes Bank, 2020

is distinguishing themselves as either for the lower class, middle class, or the consumers of Jockey which are able to pay a higher price than paying for the rest of the brands.

Similarly, if we talk about footwear, on the one hand, we have Bata, which offers office chappals and formal shoes in the name of Hush Puppies; there are companies such as Adidas and Puma which are charging more and are offering premium products to premium consumers. If we look at the opposite side of the consumer segment, Relaxo Footwear sells low-cost chappals and casual sports shoes with the brand name Sparx. If you open Amazon on your mobile and search for Hawai chappals, you will find that Relaxo has the lowest price offering and have a set quality standard for the products they are delivering.

Now let us consider India's most consumed items, tea/ coffee. Even though the coffee market is growing, the tea market is huge, and there are many tea lovers. Now when you look at this market, you will be able to bifurcate amongst the tea users based on the needs and places at which they want.

Let's say you are having Tata Tea, the black tea[25] available at a tea stall. When you go to the tea stall, you will find that you are paying Rs 10 for a cup of tea, someplace you might find it for Rs 30 because the vendor is using Amul Gold to make the tea, whereas the others are using Amul Shakti, now having product differentiation you will find that some

---

25 I am using Tata Tea as an example because Tata tea is a brand of Tata Consumer products and is listed on the stock exchanges whereas there are other private players whose tea many of us consume.

companies are catering to different segments such as giving tea made of full leaves such as Tata Darjeeling wonder rare tea and so on. In offices, you would find green tea and dip-dip that is available in different flavours. Similarly, there is Brook Bond Red Label and Wagh Bakri which is catering into different segments of the consumers.

The suppliers or the producers are giving similar kind of products, but with slight differentiation amongst them.

Oligopoly

Oligopoly is the complete opposite of monopoly business. Few players exist in the market and take up the majority of the share in the market. The companies here in this segment may or may not have pricing power depending on the industry and the type of company they are. Industries such as cement, steel, aluminium, automobiles are a few examples of the oligopolistic markets.

If we have a look into the automobile industry, we will find that there are only a few players considering different segments. Such as, in two-wheeler geared vehicles, there is Bajaj, Hero, Honda, Royal Enfield, Yamaha and even Suzuki. These companies take the majority of the market and are providing various segments of their vehicles according to different engines.

Now the main thing which you might see is that the consumers have almost no pricing power, and the price range of similar vehicles will be in the same range.

Even in the cement industry, price of the cement is the same, and there is a cartel wherein the price is determined, and the competitors have the same price. In cement, if we consider normal Portland cement, which is used widely, there is no product differentiation but a different marketing strategy, different geographical areas in which a particular company might have a strong presence and nothing more than that. The difference is between the CAPEX and the production capacity the company has. Such as because of marketing, we regularly see the ads of Ultratech Cement, and the first thing that comes to our mind while purchasing the cement would be to buy the brand of which we have heard about in the advertisement.

Now there is an interesting business which is of the airline. Here, the majority of the cost is of the airplane and is a business wherein CAPEX is required in large amounts. This also comes in oligopoly business, and even refinery business wherein there are few players such as Reliance Industries, Oil India, ONGC and a few more which constitute as the market. Even the byproduct of these businesses is being used in various industries, such as packaging; then there is jet fuel, waxes, petrochemical feedstock, lubricating oil and asphalt, which are used in different industries.

Besides all this, there is a substantial increase in oligopoly market in India, wherein 20-25 companies take majority of the profits.[26]

---

26 Dipak Mondal, 2021

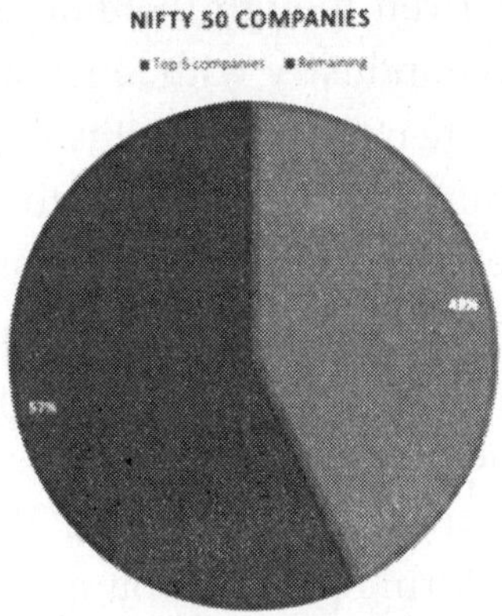

Image Source: NSE Data, Own Research

If you even look at the data, then you will find that the top five companies in the Nifty 50 are taking almost 57% of the profits, whereas the remaining are taking 43% of the profits.

Company	NP Rs.(in Cr.)
TCS	38,187.00
Tata Steel	33,011.18
Reliance Industries	31,944.00
State Bank of India	31,675.98
HDFC Bank	31,116.53

Table: The table shows the top 5 companies and their net profits. (Data collected from NSE)

Over the past few years and even because of COVID-19, we can see that the companies which were surmounting to huge debt either got dissolved or were divested, or some entered into insolvency proceeds, such as Reliance Communications arm Reliance Infratel was acquired by Reliance Jio InfoComm.

Currently, in brick-and-mortar stores, there is More megastore by Aditya Birla Group, Jio mart, Reliance retail and DMart, wherein Jio Mart has a major advantage because of Reliance retail. Even though there are small players, the concentration of the industry with few players only is going to happen as and when the adaptability of Indian consumers to order from online stores is going to increase, and the number of internet users is going to increase.

Even in the telecom industry, because of increasing competition, only three private players remain, which have the majority of the market share in terms of the number of subscribers. Tatas merged with Airtel, Vodafone and Idea merged together, forming VI, RComm and Aircel merged with Reliance Telecom.

Soon we will see more concentration of only a few players remaining, and the rest will be acquired, merged or would proceed to bankruptcy. I am not discussing the perfect competition market as, in my view, for listed companies, I do not find any perfect competitive market where all of them have an equal share, and they do not have pricing power over the products. Even in the case of identical products such as sweets, the local brand has the power to price their products differently because of certain differentiation, as well as the majority of the Indian market is still an unorganized market.

Now, as we have understood the types of market structures, it is also necessary to understand the types of companies, and how their stock prices perform, and even in which stage they are!

Growth Companies

These types of companies are usually in their nascent stage of business and, thus, are able to achieve faster growth because of a large market and capital infusion. For example, Adani

Green which was founded in 2015 has increased its assets and has grown very well. Since its listing on the exchanges, it has risen from the listing price of Rs 28.9 to Rs 2440[27]. This is where we find tenbaggers which multiplies our money.

These types of companies are high-risk and high-reward, as they are still small and trying to grow. If you wish to invest in these types of companies, then you should look for small-cap companies that have the potential to become mid-cap companies in the near future as well as have strong fundamentals supporting their business. If they fall in the monopoly segment even for a certain product, then it is worth looking for.

Cyclicals

These types of companies have their profits rise and fall according to the economic situation the country is facing. Mostly the automobile companies and the refineries fall into this category.

You might have seen during the COVID-19 time that only FMCG stocks were growing, and the rest were facing the heat because consumers were saving their income in speculation of the second Covid wave and not making expenditure. Even the crude price went negative[28];this happened because the world was in lockdown and there was no demand. Well, this is the extreme case I am talking about, but usually, when there is a recession, the consumer tends to spend less and save more, thus reducing the demand. As the majority of these businesses require a minimum amount of demand, the lower demand impacts the profitability of the companies.

---

27 Dt 19/08/2022

28 Amit Mudgill, 2022

During boom periods, these types of companies usually outperform the benchmark because the consumers' standard of living has increased, and they are willing to spend more. It also happens that there is a waiting period of more than 6-7 months which many of us might have faced. This is because of the excessive demand for the product and the limited supply that the manufacturer has.

Turnarounds

These are the types of companies which are down in the dumpster i.e., having their stock prices almost coming near zero, but you think that they might perform well because they might be able to do right during their difficult times and might be able to start generating profits.

The things which we usually look around in a turnaround are that the company has acted plans to improve its standing, the company has plans that are working, the company is removing its non-core business, or it is divesting its units which are into losses and going back to its core business and infusing capital which is very well funded.

If we look for an example, then I think Yes Bank is one of the turnaround companies because there is a change in management, whatever plan they are using is working, and they are also able to raise capital to meet the requirements for the banks.

Asset Plays

These are those types of companies that have substantial assets, but their valuation or the market rate is difficult to get, and the value of the asset is usually not reflected in the stock prices.

In India, if we look at the Godrej family, which is currently in the news because of the splitting of the property they own. This 124-year-old company owns 3400-acre land in Mumbai, and the Vikhroli land has the development potential of Rs 1 lakh crores.[29] The Godrej Properties has a market value of Rs 38,246 crores[30], and now some of the family members are planning to cash from it.

So, when you look at this land parcel, it becomes clear that the value of the land is not being shown in the current market valuation of Godrej Properties.

Stalwarts

These are those companies that are fundamentally strong and show the power to resist the market turbulence. These are usually established companies which compound their earnings usually at 10-12% per annum. Companies such as Asian Paints, Nestle, Pidilite Industries, Relaxo Footwears and many more are all known as stalwarts.

These companies have strong fundamentals and have shown outstanding growth even during turbulent times, making them resilient, which are able to pass on any type of cost to the consumers rather than decreasing their margins.

Stalwarts example	Revenue	CFO	FCF	ROCE (avg.)	Share Price
Tata Consultancy Services	11%	12%	11%	54%	15%
Infosys	10%	10%	11%	34%	19%
Asian Paints	10%	12%	13%	42%	21%
HDFC Bank	14%	NA	18%	18%	19%
Relaxo Footwear	9%	19%	38%	28%	36%

Data Source: Own Research, Ace Equity

29 John, 2021

30 Dt: 19/08/2022

Looking at the above image[31] you understand that the companies mentioned are able to compound their revenues more than the GDP growth and have a higher ROCE[32] than majority of the companies which results into higher share price compounding.

These companies have shown resilience during the last eight years because in 2014, when the new government, which is still present, came into power, and we saw financialization, the government pushed the banks to open Jan Dhan accounts which facilitated zero balance savings accounts and led to the tremendous growth of the accounts.

In 2016, we saw demonetization wherein the country faced a cash crunch and the majority of the consumers started using digital payment methods such as Paytm, Google Pay and PhonePe, with UPI volumes starting to grow, but also leading to less consumer spending and less demand from the consumers.

In June 2017, we had GST implementation, which ultimately changed the whole scenario of doing business as well as the laws regarding creating the e-way bill, which impacted many businesses and led to a slowdown of the economy.

In 2018, we technically went into recession for a few months. It was the time when the consumers started facing a

31 The data is from FY 14-22 considering eight years and even the Covid-19 period performance is included.
Note: The CFO which mentions NA is because it is banking stock and the concept of cash flow from operations is not applicable.

32 ROCE is the return on capital employed which is the total capital which one takes, own equity plus the borrowings.
Note: For HDFC Bank, Return of Equity is calculated instead of ROCE because it is a banking stock.

pinch on their pockets as businesses were not picking up on the retail or the consumer side.

Just when all these things were happening in 2019, we were faced with the challenge of lockdown, and the whole country came to a standstill. Currently, as the scenario has improved, all of us started to wonder what happened to the stock market as there was too much volatility.

Looking at the stalwart stocks, they showed growth according to their characteristics and compounded the wealth of investors over the period of eight years and will continue to do so because of the strong fundamentals they have.

Slow Growers

Slow growers are the types of companies which have reached their maturity stage, and such companies also showcase slow price growths in the market.

Companies such as ONGC, Power Grid Corporation of India, Vedanta and Gail are some of the companies which are also known as Laggards. These companies usually provide attractive dividend yields, and we should not expect too much capital appreciation.

There are even some companies that give dividends many times a year, with good dividend yields for the investors. These companies are usually invested by mutual funds, which provides monthly income plan wherein there might be hybrid plan where the mutual fund invests in such equities as well as in debt fund.

Resilient India

You all have read how from 2014-2021, there were many problems which India faced during the Modi government,

I have a Resilient India portfolio wherein the stock returns are calculated for the time period of this difficult times as mentioned in the Stalwarts segment of this chapter.

Resilient India stocks comparison to Index (FY 14-22)

Resilient India Stocks	Revenue	CFO	FCF	ROCE (avg.)	Share Price
Tata Consultancy Services	11%	12%	11%	54%	15%
Bajaj Finance	22%	NA	24%	19%	52%
Infosys	10%	10%	11%	34%	19%
LTI	12%	17%	14%	50%	54%
Asian Paints	10%	12%	13%	42%	21%
V-Mart Retail	8%	39%	NM	24%	33%
Titan Company	8%	29%	27%	27%	25%
HDFC Bank	14%	NA	18%	18%	19%
Kotak Mahindra	15%	NA	21%	13%	21%
HDFC Life Insurance Companies	7%	NA	6%	18%	3%
ICICI Lombard General Insurance Companies	18%	NA	14%	21%	16%
Nestle India	5%	4%	1%	83%	15%
Adani WIlmar	12%	21%	30%	20%	NA
Marico	7%	27%	21%	35%	19%
Tata Elxsi	13%	16%	22%	52%	47%
GMM Pfaudler	32%	43%	31%	22%	52%
Relaxo Footwear	9%	19%	38%	28%	36%
Page Industries	11%	32%	40%	62%	21%
Pidilite	6%	15%	17%	35%	25%
Median	11%	18%	19%	28%	21%
Nifty	4%	13%	26%	6%	11%

Note: ICICI securities price have been calculated for just 4 years, as it was not listed, but the data is available. i. The companies which show NA in the CFO are banking and financial companies as there is the concept of CFO does not stat valid. ii. In FCFF in banking stocks, PAT is used and instead of ROCE, ROE as a percentage is used. iii. The returns are mentioned as CAGR other than ROCE. ROCE is measured as an average. iv. For those companies, where the base year values are negative, I have taken FY 2013 data. v. Share price is not applicable for Adani Wilmar, as it has not been even a year, thus, excluded from calculating it.

Data Source: Own Research, Ace Equity, Financial Reports

I have compared all these stocks to Nifty 50 Index and have calculated the share price return. You can see that Nifty has provided 11% CAGR return whereas on a median basis also, Resilient India portfolio has generated 21% CAGR returns. It is not to boast, but when you look at the companies, these are the companies or the industries which I understand. Majority of them are consumer facing industries which serves retail customers like you and me even though they might be using different distribution channels and different modes of operations of approaching the customer and have expertise in the process wherein they can reduce the cost.

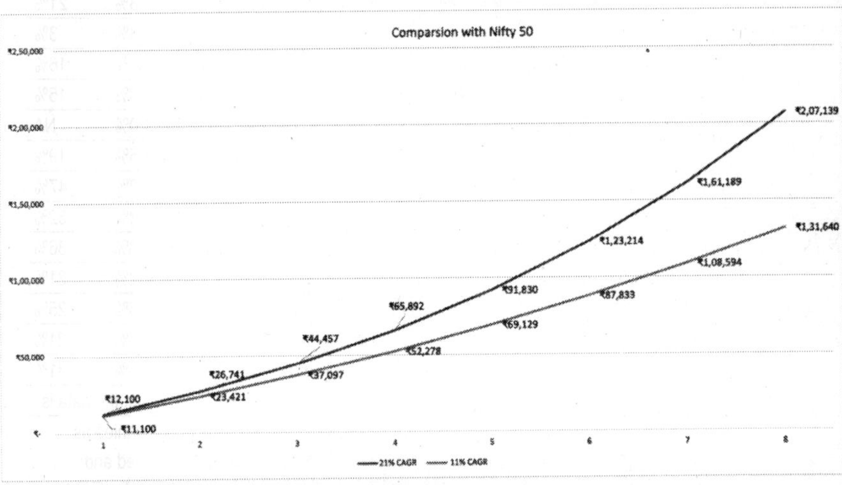

Had you invested in the above-mentioned stocks and have done SIP of Rs 10000 annually for the eight years from 2014-2022, you would have made Rs 2,07,139 whereas if you remained invested and did SIP in any of the Nifty 50 Index fund you would have made Rs 1,31,640. The dividends which you might have earned during this period would be an add-on to these results.

Thus, I believe that all the understanding of the market structures, investing in companies or the sectors which you know would generate better returns and even in those selecting good companies would make a difference to your returns as showcased in the image above.

7.
Questions to ask for self analysis

We always think of ourselves as a rational investor who is investing because we know about the company. Rather if we look into ourselves, we find that as a consumer, we are rational consumers who will bargain while purchasing things, who will look at the quality, the brand image as well as we will ask for reviews from our friends or relatives who might have bought the product or know someone who might have bought and shared the experience. But when it comes to stocks selection, we are ready to listen to a stranger in a train, bus or even at different paan shops giving investing advise and telling us to invest in a particular stock, and then after coming home, many of us invest in that stock.

The problem with this approach is that different individuals have different goals; some might want to save for their child's education, the others might be saving for the marriage of their daughter or son, or might want to buy a house within a certain time period.

What the majority of us forget is that even if we get one of the best stock recommendations, the holding period, the risk capacity, the goals, and the investment ideology is totally different for all the individual investors, as well as the timing of entry and exit would be different. So, there are certain questions that one needs to ask themselves to understand their goals better and fulfil them according to one's risk appetite.

Why are you investing?

This is the main question, as to why you are investing in equities or even doing SIPs in mutual funds. Without the answer to this question, there are chances that you might not remain invested in for a longer period of time, or you might panic and sell when the markets are not doing good according to your expectations.

Not knowing the reason why you are investing is the most dangerous thing one can do. The time horizon will depend on your answer only.

Can you reinvest in the same company?

Assume you invested in a mutual fund without thinking ahead and then after some time you might need funds, for emergency or you must have forgotten a particular major expense coming up? Or taking the best-case scenario, you are thinking of profit booking. Will you sell when it is in the highs, or a boom period is going on? After selling during the highs, are you going to buy when the price of the share has increased?

Let me share you an example; my father owns Tata Elxsi at an average price of Rs 902 and he sells at assume Rs 1200. After selling the share, the share price goes up another Rs 300 within a month because of good performance. Now, will you be able to buy the same share at Rs 1500 or will you wait for some time for the share to fall? Another question that comes up while you are thinking is that will it fall in the next month and how much will it fall? Are you sure you will still be able to buy during that dip?

What would you do if the scenario was worst case – you own the stock, there is dip in the stock, will you do average of the stock? Is there any money left with you or will you wait more for the stock to fall? Majority of the investors who have lost their money is by not investing into a particular stock and just thinking about all these questions which I just mentioned.

What is your investment time horizon?

Rather than thinking about how much you can invest monthly or annually, what matters more is the investment time horizon and then selecting the investment instrument accordingly.

Just imagine that you are in your 20s and have started a job or a business of your own. You will have some profit or salary saved, from which you might want secure returns. So, if you are saving a certain amount, then you can also have a time period of thirty years in future. For someone in their 50s, they will have ten years' time horizon if they are planning to retire by the age of sixty and would be opting for an annuity plan which might give them regular income as and when the investor retires from the job.

Now imagine you do not wish to take the risk and wish to remain invested for only 1-2 years, but you choose to invest in the ELSS[33] mutual fund, which has a lock-in period of three years. Now that you have made a wrong investment decision, your money is also stuck, and you might require to borrow from the bank or someplace else. There are different instruments to

---

33 Equity Linked Savings Scheme

invest in for different time periods. Bonds are there, mutual funds are there, direct equity investment is there.

Even though I do not recommend it, there are instances when there are merger events or when corporations are doing share buybacks and are prepared to take it at a higher price than the current market price, and you can trade it for a short amount of time as you are taking the fixed return way. On 12 Jan 2022, TCS[34] announced buyback of its share, the market price of its share was Rs 3807.42. The company said that it will buy back the share at the price of Rs 4500 per share and will start doing it from 9 March 2022 till 23 March 2022. So, you can think of booking profits in such cases because the risk of loss is minimum to none.

On the other hand, there are times when merger talks are going on or else some listed company wants to take over another company. We all have read about the growth of Adani, when the news of Adani taking entire stake of Holcim India was out, the shares of ACC cement and Ambuja cement rose[35] up by 10% but soon tanked also because Adani pledged[36] those shares. All these events happened between a span of three days. On 19 September 2022, ACC and Ambuja rose by 10% and on 21 September 2022, both ACC and Ambuja tanked by more than 7%.

This thing seems risky, but then again, luck plays a role on the individual investor and the choice in which the person wants to take risk, depending on the time horizon he/she wants for their expected returns. This is the reason I always suggest

34 TCS Buyback 2022, 2022

35 Aseem Thapiyal, 2022

36 Surbhi Jain, 2022

for long term investing rather than trading and looking for short term opportunities because we do not have time to grasp all this information regarding the events that are taking place in the markets because of job or business which you are doing.

Is there a need for a regular income?

Do you have any need for a regular income? Some might have and some might not, for someone who is doing a job might not require regular income and can invest in equities and gain capital appreciation by investing in good companies.

Now, I have seen many retail investors go after the companies which give good dividends. All those companies are usually slow growers and have a dividend yield of somewhere around 5-10%, but the thing which I have seen is that their total investment does not exceed more than five lacs in equities, but their long-term investment might exceed in instruments such as PPF.

For a person who is in the 20s or 30s, in my opinion, it makes no sense to keep the majority of their investments which might provide you certain kinds of dividends. Even you are even earning 10 lacs per annum and invest 10% of your savings because there are different obligations which need to be fulfilled, you are investing 1 lac per annum and best case 2 lacs per annum. Out of that, when you invest in high yield companies you are getting the most Rs 20000 per annum.

This amount will probably not impact your lifestyle because you have a primary source of income wherein you can compound at a minimum rate of 11%[37].

---

37 Sensex has compounded at 11% over the last minimum ten years.

What can be considered as risk according to you?

A different individual can have a different risk appetite, and you might not understand the stock market at all and still invest in different financial instruments. Stock market seems risky to most because of lack of understanding of financial markets as well as having almost zero financial knowledge to understand what all instruments are there in the markets.

Let's assume you have a low-risk appetite because you might think that investing in equities is risky. So you have made your investments in gold and real estate, and you are also making an investment in PPF[38] or NPS[39] schemes. Even investing in Sensex might seem risky to some individuals, so they just leave them and rather focus on the fixed income instruments.

Now, on the other side, if you understand stock markets as well as can read financial statements, then you would be willing to take the risk of getting returns somewhere around 15% and investing in different types of ETFs, mutual funds or investing directly into stocks.

There is another type of person, the one who understands the market but is not in a position to lose any capital or does not have the capacity to take the risk, either because of their personality or the background conditions in which they are currently. Some investors might have other expenses ahead of them or look out for the needs of their families.

---

38 Public Provident Fund

39 National Pension Scheme

Such types of investors can invest in debt as well as equity to balance out.

Which type of Industry do you understand?

If I talk about myself, even though I don't understand every industry and its functioning, the same goes for the majority of the investors. It is almost impossible for a single person to understand every type of industry.

Some of you might be working in aviation, some in logistics, and some in FMCG. These are just examples, but it is best to invest in companies from the industry you understand because whenever there are economic or even company-level changes, you would be able to understand easily and won't make the mistake of selling or exiting at the wrong price level.

Many of you might be business owners, so it may be easy for you to understand the economic impacts of your sector, because even your business is likely to get affected by the changes. So, I would suggest you stick to 3-4 industries which you understand rather than investing in any company which you might have heard from someone else, which gave them good returns for a specific time period. It makes no sense to invest in pharma companies when you are good at understanding FMCG and other consumer facing business. This is just like investing by listening from a stranger.

Is there any regular income need from your investments?

This is an essential question to ask yourself. As you know that India is a country wherein the per capita income is $2000.

It can be considered that the majority of the Indians are in the lower middle-class category.

So, if you don't have the need for regular income from the investments that you have made, it is better to invest for the period you have set to achieve your goal and invest in those companies which give you better returns.

It turns out that when you don't require regular income from the investments, then you should not make profit booking because you are going to lose returns from the investments, and real returns will actually be less.

Particulars	Buy	Sell	Quantity	Profit %
Equity X	₹1,000.00	₹1,200.00	₹ 100.00	
Profit			₹ 20,000.00	20.00%
Charges				
Brokerage			₹-	
STT[40] Total			₹ 220.00	
Exchange txn charges			₹ 7.59	
DP[41] charge			₹15.93	
GST			₹1.37	
SEBI charges			₹ 0.26	
Stamp Duty			₹15.00	
Total Tax and charges			₹ 260.15	
Net Profit			₹ 19,739.85	
STCG[42] charges		15%	₹ 2,960.98	
Net Realisable Gain			₹ 16,778.87	16.11%

As I am using Zerodha for trading, I am calculating the same with their brokerage calculator.

40 Securities Transaction Tax

41 Depository Participant Charges

42 Short Term Capital Gains Tax

As you can see that the above table depicts how profit booking reduces the profits, we can see that for an investor who doesn't need regular income, it's a loss of almost 3.5%. For those investors who need regular income from investing won't be considering this minimum loss that much as much as a regular investor.

Even if you invest in a different company which gives you the same amount of return, you will be losing out on real gains because of STCG[43], but there is also a probability that you might invest in a company which is not going to give you expected returns of 20% on annual basis; you only get somewhere between 12-15%. So again, you are at a loss. What would have happened if you booked profit from TCS and then invest in company like Vodafone Idea or even Yes Bank?

How much negative are you willing to go?

There are chances that your investments might go negative for a particular year. It will never be that your investments will always go up every year. There are chances that your portfolio might go into the red and then come up again in green in a year.

Would you panic sell at that moment, or would you rather understand the scenario and wait for things to settle down? Many investors panic and sell because they don't know much about the fundamentals of the company, or don't understand how the particular industry works.

Many investors love their companies and keep them even when there is something wrong with the fundamentals, and the company is going into bankruptcy. Still, they are willing

---

43 Day traders need not pay attention to this question.

to hold on to such companies assuming that it might go up someday or in order to average their losses.

Assume you invested in Future group, and then it went into turmoil as it is now. For how long are you willing to hold? Isn't it better to remove such companies from your portfolio rather than wait for a long period of time and invest in companies that have been consistently compounding your money? This would reduce your losses over a longer period of time, as you have reduced the holding period, which were giving you negative returns.

Which type of company would you like to invest in?

Would you like to invest in companies which are blue chip companies such as HDFC Bank, Asian Paints, TCS, Infosys, Reliance and many more and have less risk, considering that they are sort of market leaders in their segments? Or invest in companies which are in small-cap and medium cap and you think they have the potential to become a midcap company or a large cap company, respectively?

There are high risks and high returns. Are you comfortable in investing in new age tech companies such as Paytm, Zomato, India Mart and Nykaa, some of which are into losses. Or the above-mentioned blue-chip companies which are having consistent cashflows and are into profits?

Do you mind if the companies in which you want to invest have large amounts of debt, such as the Adani Green, or you would want debt free company such as Reliance?

Understand which type of investor you are and which types of companies you are willing to invest in based on the filters which you create.

Are you doing re-assessment?

Many investors have exit strategies predefined over a time horizon. It may be different for different investors, but it is there, or you can say that it is deciding your goal before investing and then selecting the investment instrument. It is similar to the first self-analysis question that I asked you.

Once you have defined your exit strategy, you would have given the time period. Then it is always recommended that you reanalyze your strategy because there are chances that you might be over expecting or under expecting from the investments that you have made.

Rewrite your goals every year and make investment decisions accordingly. Keep on tracking whether they are deviating from your return requirements positively or negatively or are they in line with your expectations.

If it's a bad company, you are anyway going to lose money even if you do averaging in the same company. You might just not get out of the company and remain invested in the bad one because you might have fallen in love with the company and are not letting go of one bad investment for the sake of earning from others. You are anyways losing on returns by not investing in a good company.

8.
Investing step by step

In this chapter, I will discuss the investment ideology I have and the steps or analyses I have followed and learned over time. To be frank, I am in my 20s, and I have a business running out of which I earn my regular income. Therefore for me, there is no need to invest in companies which are giving good dividends, but rather the companies which are giving strong compounding over a period of time wherein I have a thirty-year time horizon.

Even if I do SIPs and invest just Rs 10,000 per month over thirty years with an average which I expect i.e., 15% compounding, I would have invested only 36 lacs, but the value of my investments would be somewhere around 7 Cr. This would benefit me in a way that my investment value would have been averaged because, over the years, I would have invested in both the ups and downs in the markets.

There are two approaches I use – the top to bottom approach and the bottom-up approach. Ultimately, the bottom-up approach will be useful because it talks about the company and not the economy, which is constantly changing over time. For me, it is all about the company – whether the company is able to adapt to the current situation and remain stable in crisis periods and over a longer time horizon and how the company has changed and added new income streams either organically or inorganically.

Top to bottom approach

Let me start with the first approach, I will explain the few things I look at and how they impact. But, understand one thing, the top to bottom approach is not to look at things daily and take actions accordingly, but it has to be looked over a span of years and how things have changed and try to understand how things can change by either reading or talking to others.

Rate of Interest

I look at the rate of interest set by the banks and the RBI to understand whether they are expanding money flow into the markets or trying to decrease it. You might have seen that after Covid-19 restrictions were lifted, the RBI reduced the repo rates and took an expansionary stance in order to make consumers spend more. That's because when interest rates come down, the cost of capital is also decreased, and the businesses are willing to expand and can expand more easily by borrowing, as well as the consumers can also take loans.

As already mentioned, I don't look at the rate of interest on a daily basis, but rather once every quarter or just listen to the interview of MPC,[44] it gives me information which makes it easier to understand what is going on in the economy.

Also, as I have invested in the banking and NBFC companies, the companies are also impacted by them in the short and long term. Understanding the rate of interest gives me a cost of capital for the companies which are listed as well as for non-listed businesses. There are certain industries

---

44 Monetary Policy Committee

which might not be impacted because of an increase in cost of capital. This is due to the nature of their business, because they can pass it on to the end consumers. Even in my packaging industry, I can pass it on to my companies if there is any increase or decrease in the cost of capital. Similar thing happens in cable and broadcasting industry; it is still semi organized, and many small players are there, which are not impacted by interest rate changes.

Bond Yields

This gives me information about the preference of investors, whether the demand for the bond is high or the investors are pumping money into equity markets. When there is high demand for bonds, it tells us about the investor sentiment that investors are not willing to take more risk and invest in equities, which might also impact the share price of the stocks on a temporary basis and gives me an opportunity to purchase the stock which I think is good.

I also like to look at these to understand the risk-free rate of interest, as in without taking any risk I am going to get 'x' amount of returns if I invest in government bonds.

Sector Contribution to GDP, Imports and Exports

This is one of the important factors which I need to consider while looking at the sectors. Here, I study historical data, the trends that have changed and the reason for their change. Are we repeating the same history, or is there a new thing or phenomenon that is happening in the market?

From looking at the figures, I can identify and verify what all things are happening in the industry by observing and then making speculations about what all can happen considering the past.

I always believe that humans are going to repeat history because of their nature of greed and keep on making the same mistakes in a different style. We know of the dot-com bubble and the 2008 financial crisis because of greed. There are different crises, but these two are famous and even are taught in schoolbooks, especially the dot-com bubble.

I make a great deal about understanding what caused them, what was the scenario of imports and exports done by India at that time, whether we went into recession or we managed, and our country was not impacted that much. If our country was cushioned somehow, what were the reasons behind it? All these things make me understand where our country is going and reduces the noise made by the rating agencies as well as different political parties where they might see something else happening.

Even though the things mentioned above in this segment are to be seen on quarterly or semi-annual basis, I believe it is absolute necessity to understand sector contribution as well as industry growth rates. If you look at the industry of tobacco, many countries all over the globe are wanting to reduce tobacco usage, so we can see it is a declining industry. Companies in this industry face such hurdles while growing. I cannot expect companies to be growing at 10-15% annually if the industry is declining.

Similarly, when you look at the overall competition in the globe, India is the fifth largest economy and thus, India is not a small cap player, rather a large cap. So even different businesses will have competitive advantage in different countries. If you see textile industry, you cannot expect Indian companies to compete as good as those in Vietnam or Bangladesh. The sole reason is availability of cheap labour, exchange rate difference between India and the other countries. On a similar side, it would be difficult for other countries to have competitive advantage when it comes to business process outsourcing. wherein it would be very difficult to beat companies like TCS.

Government Agenda for the country

This is very important as when the government starts promoting something or comes out with a policy. they are promoting that particular sector and doing business in that sector is easier.

For example, the government came up with production-linked incentives (PLI schemes) as well as they are promoting *Atmanirbhar Bharat Abhiyan*. As a business and even as an investor, I understand that the government wants more businesses to set up their manufacturing and servicing units in India. Then I look at what all sectors will be impacted and try to figure out what can be the areas where there can be an upside demand more than some sectors, which sectors will be impacted negatively, if there are some companies which are negatively impacted, are they doing something for that?

Is this just happening in India, or is the phenomenon all over the world? If you have been reading news on a regular basis, you would understand that during the 90s, we opened up our economy to the world, bringing liberalization. Not just us, every other country all over the world was making efforts to make the world economy an open economy wherein trade could be made easily.

As the things have moved forward coming to the present scenario, every country is thinking of becoming independent and is focusing on developing their own country rather than being totally dependent on the global economy. You might have seen the famous campaign done by Donald Trump, who was president of the United States. We have an ongoing campaign done by our Prime Minister Narendra Modi, called Atmanirbhar Bharat.

Even various schemes are going on in the US and other countries to start manufacturing in their home countries and not just certainly become dependent on the others.

These are the few things which tell me what is going on overall in the economy, and other than just reading the news, sometimes listening to the podcast, experts over YouTube, listening to different CEOs about how they think where the economy is going and how they perceive it over short and longer periods of time.

Considering all these things, they will take a lot of time, and I understand that most of you might not understand everything or even have an interest in reading all these things, but just want to focus on finding good companies. So, there, I use the bottom-up approach. I request all those who are reading to get familiar with a few terms or certain important ratios which can be used while understanding whether the company is good or not.

Bottom-Up Approach

In this approach, the first thing I look at is the product list which they are selling in order to identify the end consumers. Sometimes the product list is vast, but that is okay; you might have heard about the product, or chances are you might be the customer. If we talk about the company such as Marico, I am their end user as I am using their edible oil, which is the Saffola brand and even the hair oil, which is the Parachute brand.

Doing this step helps me in identifying the consumer type and even the broad psychology of the consumers they are providing their product to, and the demand can be predicted, not in quantity, but the impact in case of some unlikely event such as the Covid-19 that happened.

Management Discussion and Auditors' report

I like to read management discussion even though it might not give an accurate picture, but it definitely gives some hint of the demand they forecast as well as some companies even discuss the global scenario which might have impacted them or the local scenario which might have impacted them.

The majority of the companies do a SWOT[45] analysis and tell us where they see opportunities as well as threats. I like to read the chairman's message, which they usually write. Most importantly, the auditor's report, which gives its opinion while analyzing the company and gives its qualified[46] or

---

45 Strength, Weaknesses, Opportunity, Threats

46 It means that the auditor finds the report fairly represented with the exception of the identified areas.

unqualified[47] opinion of the company, which can give the investor a green or a red flag depending on the opinion.

Even for companies that are filing for IPOs, you will find such report in the DRHP[48] and can analyze whether to invest in IPO or not.

P/E ratio

Though some investors argue that the P/E ratio is not that useful, sometimes, I beg to differ. When you look at the industry P/E ratio, you will understand the investor sentiment as to how much they are willing to pay for the earnings.

If you are to find good companies, the historical P/E data, which can be averaged or even just looking at the historical P/E ratios, you will get to understand a certain range in which the stock usually keeps on playing. Also, it is not just earnings, but many a time, even P/E ratio expands, and investors are willing to pay for the same stock more.

Why? Because an analyst might have taken note of it, or some big investor or fund might have invested in it and then every other investor is looking to invest in it. Sometimes it is altogether a new segment, such as climate change; you might have seen the P/E of Adani Green which has the P/E ratio of 827, meaning that people are willing to pay 827 times the current earnings.

In short, if everything remains the same, such as the earnings remaining the same, it will take you 827 years to recover or get that much that you have paid over time. The

47 It means that the auditor finds the report fairly represented without identified exemptions.

48 Draft Red Herring Prospectus which is submitted to SEBI.

best thing to do is to look at the companies which are not that much covered by analysts as well as look for the companies which are in second or third place in earnings, but have almost similar ratios as compared to the largest company and are functioning in a similar manner.

For example, when we look at TCS, Infosys, Mind Tree, and LTI, there will be differences in their P/E, and chances are you might get one of the good companies at a discounted price because analysts are not tracking it but still giving good returns.

Earnings per share

This is one of the important things I usually look at and see what percentage it has grown, whether it is compounding at 5%, 10% or more. It is more important for me to look at EPS compounding than P/E because if we look at the share price, the price changes when there is a change in EPS which is multiplied by a change in the P/E ratio.

For example, the share price is Rs 100 now, and the P/E, as well as the EPS, is 10. Now, if my EPS goes to 11 and P/E remains the same, the share price will be Rs 110 and will keep on compounding. So even if someday my P/E is reduced, the overall impact will be less against only P/E growing.

Particulars	Price	P/E	EPS
Year 1	100.00	10	10
Year 2	112.00	10	11.20
Year 3	125.44	10	12.54
Year 4	140.49	10	14.05
Year 5	157.35	10	15.74
Year 6	176.23	10	17.62

Particulars	Price	P/E	EPS
Year 7	197.38	10	19.74
Year 8	221.07	10	22.11
Year 9	247.60	10	24.76
Year 10	277.31	10	27.73
Year 11	155.29	5	31.06

In the above table, I have drawn a calculation that my EPS is compounding at 12% CAGR and the P/E remains the same for ten years, considering the economy is growing. Suddenly we face a black swan event such as Covid and my P/E slashed to half. Even though it has happened, I am not at a loss because the price is still above the price at which I invested in as well as this is for the shorter time period that my stock's P/E is reduced.

Now imagine if P/E expanded more than the earnings growth, and if something like this happened, you might be at a loss in the long term.

Return on capital employed (ROCE)

Rather than looking for ROE,[49] I prefer to look at the ROCE of the companies. This measure gives the return on overall capital that is invested, i.e. the equity, as well as the amount of money taken through loans. Many investors such as Warren Buffet, Charlie Munger and Peter Lynch, from whom I have developed the ideology regarding investing, believe that over the long term, the share price returns given by a stock are almost similar to the company's ROCE.

You cannot expect the share price returns to be more than ROCE over long term of 10-15 years.

49 When the companies are in banking or financial companies, ROE is used for measurement of returns.

Revenue and PAT growth

What is the rate at which the revenue and PAT are growing or compounding? For the return expectations that I have, I look at ten years of data and have a look that the PAT, as well as revenues, have compounded at 10% CAGR in seven years. If the companies are not able to compound at this level, then I feel that it is not growing, because considering the historical data and just for the assumption levels also, the rate of inflation is almost 6-7% and adding a country risk premium[50] of 3%, I require a minimum growth rate of 10% at company level.

Free cash flow to firm and Cash flow from operations

As I have a business, the most important thing for any business is the cash flow, the timing of it and particularly the cash flow that I generate from regular day-to-day operations. If the company is not able to compound those cashflows at a good rate or more than its peers, it will not be able to grow at a faster rate than its peers.

FCFF is a really important factor while looking at the financial statements as it represents the amount of cash the company has with itself after deducting the capital expenditures made by the company. A negative FCFF is not a good sign for the company as we may see that it is not able to generate a good amount of cash and is losing money.

---

50 Based on the extra risk which we take in comparison to developed nations.

Sometimes there can be negative FCFF for companies as they might have done capital expenditures or might have acquired some other business which is also running well and have to pay the price from it. There is another thing to look out for; good companies usually have cash flow from operations greater than their net profits. If the company is not able to maintain that level, it comes to me as a red flag.

Is it a group company?

What I have observed over the years is that group companies do not get a good valuation in terms of P/E, and their earnings are sometimes compromised. The problem that I find with group companies is that they have invested in different businesses out of which some might give fantastic results, but the others might not be able to match how the company performs.

For example, Grasim has Ultratech Cement, which is subsidiary of Grasim, the main business of Grasim is of chemicals, cellulose. There are other companies of Aditya Birla such as Aditya Birla Capital and the payments bank which I have mentioned.

All the subsidiaries like Ultratech cement, Aditya Birla capital, Cellulose Division, its clothing division won't be giving same returns and thus the group company has lesser P/E than a standalone company. Aditya Birla Capital, Aditya Birla Payments bank and many more. Not all of these companies are going to meet the return expectations as an investor, so I would better invest in individual companies and reap the benefits out of it.

Reinvestment ratio and Dividend distribution

This is also one of the important factors which I consider because if the company is giving the majority of its earnings back to the consumer, then I believe they are not finding good opportunities from which they can generate better returns on behalf of the investors. Also, I have seen that all the companies with high ROCE, usually beyond twenty, are reinvesting the FCFF and again generating a return. Take the example of Berkshire Hathaway, which has not given dividends, but has provided investors with capital appreciation. Companies such as Asian Paints, Pidilite, and Bajaj Finance also give very little dividend as a percentage; the rest is being reinvested into the business. This gives them an edge over the competitors.

Story

This is the last thing and is very important for me personally because I need to understand the story of the company without which I cannot invest in that company. If I cannot connect with the story or understand the functioning of the company or how it has its advantages over others and how it has grown, the way they have evolved or the way they beat competition and why it has been able to sustain the market position, what are their future plans.

All these things are very important to me, I usually don't invest in companies in which I cannot understand all these things even though the financials are good and I think it can give me expected returns.

Opinion

If, as an investor, you are not able to do it or are not interested in doing the research, then it is better to find an investment advisor or a good fund manager and invest with them because they will invest wisely and more actively, paying good attention and keeping your money safe.

If you wish to invest on your own without doing the research, the best option would be a low-cost index fund which will give your returns.

9.
Changing methods

Businesses have changed over the years, as has the way business is conducted. Now that I think of businesses in India, companies are coming up with IPOs which are still not profitable and are unicorn businesses in their respective field because of the investments they received from private equity. In this chapter, I will be valuing a new age tech company as well as a traditional company that has been in business even before I was born and will also discuss new things that are coming up in the market which may change the method of how businesses are done in e-commerce and traditional space of doing business.

Earlier, there used to be simplicity in understanding different businesses as the sales used to tell us many details; even companies were majorly in the manufacturing or service industry. The total number of products sold in every segment was enough to provide us the information we required.

Nowadays, I find it difficult to value new-age tech companies which may or may not be profitable, and I have seen the metrics of valuation changing over a period of time. The government is recognizing and telling the companies to show such KPIs[51] which they usually show the private equity investors while pitching to raise funds.

51 Key performance indicators.

Setting the table

Over the years, valuation metrics and even business models have changed. In this segment I will be talking about the changing metrics[52]and the hockey stick approach which the majority of the companies are adopting and my opinion on it.

When we used to travel, we used to look at distance in kilometers, but now, when we ask someone how far that place is? We start talking about hours or minutes. Things have changed, whether it be a flight, bus, or train, or you are going through your car. Similarly, in businesses, earlier we used to look at CAPEX and the cash flows and use the DCF method to value a company, but since the new age tech companies have little CAPEX, now we feel the need to value the customers and bring out the unit economics, which is still difficult to get because the majority of the companies are not disclosing them.

Increased requirements

What I believe is that there is a need to understand the unit economies of the new age companies, which are generally consumer-facing businesses. If I talk about Ola, Zomato or even Paytm and companies which are not listed – such as BharatPe and PhonePe – and many other such companies, I will require a few things from them.

- The number of active monthly customers.
- The number of customers who are using their services more than a year and more than five years.

---

52 Metrics of changing valuation is based on the ideology formed from the learnings of Aswath Damodaran.

- The unit economics of the consumers.
- The number of customers who are shifting to the competitors.
- The amount of advertisement expenditure done on the existing customer and the amount done to acquire new customers.
- The amount of time the customers are spending on their particular platform.

Now that we have such questions, I feel that they all need to be understood differently based on how their business is done. These are just few questions which are generalized and can be asked to every company. More questions can be added depending on the sector the company is and your understanding of the company.

Understanding of companies

While valuing the companies, there is also a need to value a customer, ultimately resulting in the company's valuation. Now the question might arise in your mind, what is the value of a company based on the user?

It is nothing but the value or the revenue which the existing user is providing, the value that the new customer might bring and subtract all the expenses incurred in order to provide the services to the users.

Usually there are three models which these new age tech companies are using.

1. **Subscription Based:** These companies are easier to value as you know that we will be focusing on ARPU[53] and

53 Average Revenue Per User

the number of active customer base the company has on monthly or even quarterly basis. Companies such as Netflix, Amazon Prime Video, Indiamart and even other OTT or news companies which are giving services based on subscription – they all fall into this category. So, if the company loses its subscribers, it will lose revenues as well as the opposite is also true. Some companies have freemium model in which few things are free, and few things come when you take the subscription. If you are using any OTT you will understand that companies like SonyLiv, Jio, Zee5 offer few things free of cost and then you would have to purchase their subscription to avail full services.

2. **Transaction Based:** These are the companies which earn their revenue based on the number of transactions the customer makes. Companies such as Zomato, Nykaa, Amazon Prime and almost all e-commerce companies or even traditional businesses[54] which have started selling online. The major metric will be 'take rates' that is the margin they are able to earn from the total sales of the products or which they write as gross merchandise value.
3. **Advertisement Based:** These companies usually scale up faster, as there is little capital to be invested. These companies usually emphasize on sale of advertising as a major source of their revenue and earn from the customers who are willing to place ads on their platform. Facebook is the prime example of this model as you can

54 A part of revenue which comes from online can be valued through the new metrics by giving appropriate weightage.

place ads on Facebook and the company makes efforts that the consumers spend as much time as possible on their platform and they collect extensive data of users and how the advertisers are going to benefit from advertising on their platform.

While learning to value a company, I understood that the company could be valued even on a piece of paper, and a good range or approximate value can be found out while drawing assumptions of what can happen to the company in a few years. Let me share with you the Paytm valuation which I did after its IPO and when its stock performance was bad as a part of my series of blogs and videos, which I called – Bleeding Unicorns.

Setting the table

We have seen Paytm growing from being just an instrument of prepaid payments and now to becoming everything from a marketplace to Demat and many more things. It has a relatively short history compared to other traditional businesses, and I believe that much of its rise is due to the smartphone revolution. So, I will start by explaining the growth drivers that are taking place and then move to Paytm.

The Indian smartphone market has grown substantially as in 2010, it was just a mere 2% of the total cellular subscription, and now there are more than 500 mn subscribers who are using smartphones.

Cellular Subscriptions from 2005 to 2020: India, China, US, EU & World

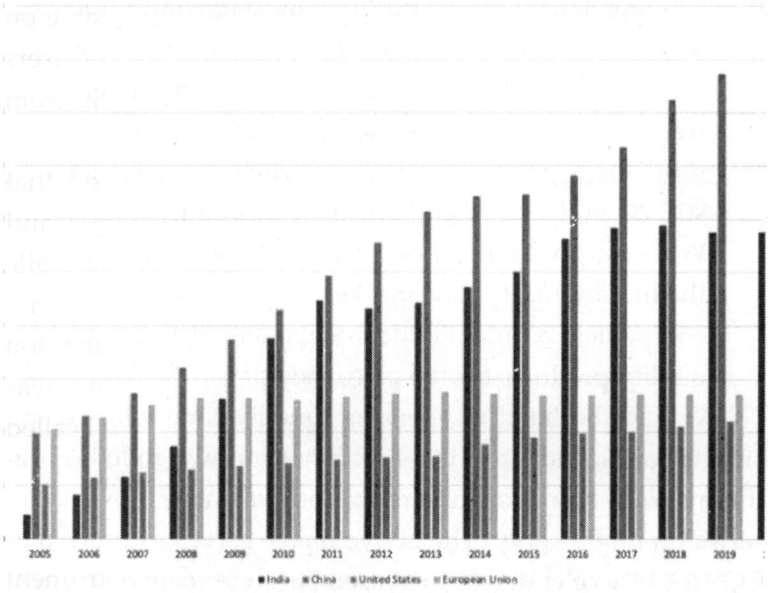

Image Source: Aswath Damodaran Blog

There are two major factors that have played a role in smartphone growth.

- Chinese companies have entered the Indian market – Oppo, Vivo and Xiaomi – where the smartphones were priced under 15K and some under 10K for Indian consumers to buy them instead of the featured phone. As well as the constant improvement in UI is one of the reasons.
- The lower cost of using mobile data and free of charge calling played a great role. I would say that it was because of Reliance, which changed the whole scenario of how telecom operators were operating. With the

launch of Jio, it was able to get 100 mn subscribers availing 4G facility in no time and launching free calls all over India. I still remember, my father used to pay for incoming calls also, and then during my time, it was free. During my time, I used to enable an SMS pack to send messages to my friends when the internet was still 2G and was costly. This was during the time when WhatsApp was also new in the market. Entering 2021, the Indian smartphone market is being ruled by Chinese companies, as mentioned earlier and still, people get quality products for the price they pay.

We had the habit of spending quality time while using smartphones, and since the 4G connection was rolled out in the market, many consumers started watching movies and series on mobile only. The above image serves as proof that COVID-19 accelerated or increased our time spent on mobile. Even though it was not only for watching series and movies, we were using it for making payments to our peers as well as the merchants through scanning QR codes.

Image Source: S&P Global Market Intelligence

Access to smartphones but poor banking reach gave rise to what we know as UPI in 2016. From there on, there was no looking backwards.

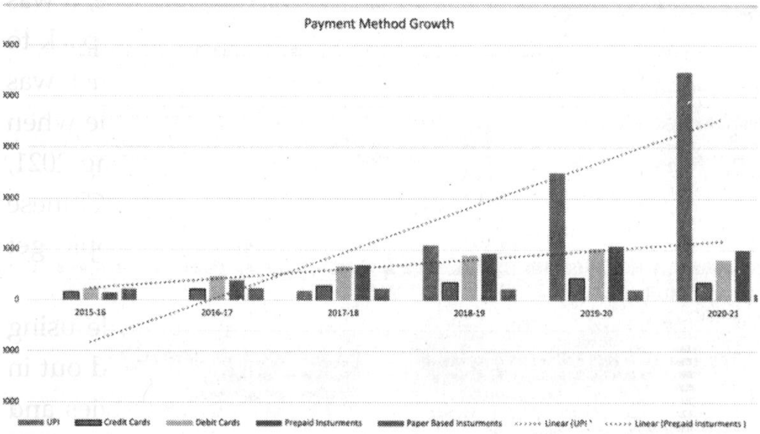

Data Source: Data collected from RBI

From 2016-17, when UPI started, the Indian consumers became acquainted with the usage of UPI, and you can see the linear growth which I have plotted in the graph. I would not have believed until I had plotted the graph from the data that after demonetisation and since the inception of UPI, the usage of cash as a method of payment has decreased.

Paytm: The story

Paytm, which meant pay through mobile, grew from 2010 to what it is now. But as the Paytm IPO came, we all saw a drastic price reduction, and while I was valuing the company and doing input for valuation, the stock price was Rs 599 per share. It is a peer-to-peer payment app with multiple offerings such as being an insurance aggregator, payments bank, small finance lending and many more. It was founded in 2010 by Vijay Sharma wherein it operated as a prepaid services provider, but its market and services were small during that time.

Now let me take you for a walk on Paytm's timeline.

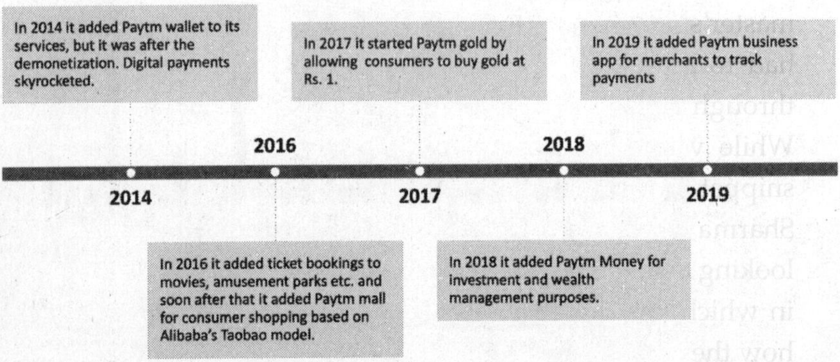

Image Source: Data collected from Paytm website

It grew its business by two things, mainly through innovations and R&D, and then through acquisitions it did of companies. While not boring you with the details of the companies it acquired, there are a few things which I have taken into consideration while valuing this company as the traditional method of using P/E multiple doesn't work, even though the world has been talking about the new methods that I have taken much care of.

- Gross Merchandise Value (GMV) is the total value of the merchandise it sold on its platform
- Take Rate is the rate of the percentage revenue it earns on GMV.
- Operating Margins

- Reinvestment as it is not possible for any company to grow without doing reinvestments.

A few days back, I was at a petrol pump and saw a Paytm box, not the soundbox but for slip printing for any transaction made either through UPI, POS or from wallets. I still remember that three years back, while I was doing my master's and paying through Paytm, the refuelling stations had to keep a person just for writing the payments made through apps, and now things have been made so smooth. While valuing the company, it became difficult to find a snippet or a comment wherein this company or even Vijay Sharma commented on making the company profitable. So looking at the past historical records and the current scenario in which they are growing, I made certain assumptions on how they may grow[55].

Valuation Story

In this segment, I will start by giving you the value drivers which I have found while studying the balance sheet and then utilising it for valuation.

55 This article was written long back on my blog called My not so Profound Thoughts. Currently while writing this book, I came to know that the assumptions which I made, that the Paytm will increase its market in lending sector to become profitable has become true.

Value Driver	Paytm's Standing	Story for the future
Gross Merchandising Value (GMV)	In 2020-21, Paytm had Rs. 4,033 billion in GMV, from its array of products & services.	Indian mobile market is expected to increase five-fold in the next five years, as smartphone penetration rises.
Market Share	Paytm dominates the person-to-merchant (P2M) business in India with a market share > 50%. It lags PhonePe and Google Pay among UPI apps.	Paytm will maintain its market share in the UPI app market, while consolidating its dominance of the P2M market.
Take Rate (Revenues as % of GMV)	Paytm's take rate has been dropping consistently over the last four years and stands at 0.79%, as company has prioritized users & transactions.	Paytm will gradually increase its take over the next 5 years to 1%, and then double that rate over the following five years (to 2%)
Operating Margin	In 2020-21, Paytm reported an operating margin of -49%, an improvement over 2019-20. Paytm's biggest expense, after employee costs, was selling & marketing, accounting for 19% of revenues.	As Paytm matures, there should be economies of scales that kick in, pushing operating margins into positive territory and beyond. By 2030, the operating margin will approach 30%.
Reinvestment	Paytm's biggest investments have been in acquisitions of companies & technology, to expand its product/service offerings.	Paytm will generate Rs.2.45 in revenues for every rupee invested, roughly in line with sales to capital ratiosfor Paypal and Square.

Note: These are the assumptions that I have taken for creating future story. There are few drivers on which I have given weightage.

As mentioned earlier, most of Paytm's and its competitors' growth was due to increased demand for smartphones and consumers' unavailability of proper banking facilities. While Paytm has an advantage in the prepaid payment method, apps such as PhonePe and Google pay have outmanoeuvred Paytm in the UPI ecosystem, which has been growing more than what we can expect.

Paytm claims that it is not just the UPI, there are other payment methods such as prepaid, debit cards, credit cards, and POS where they wish to grow. Even though they have lagged in UPI, it still has the lion's share in the prepaid method.

Now let me explain every value driver that is there.

- If we look at Paytm, it has competition from its peers not only in the Indian market but in the overall market outside India, where Paytm is not there. While we look at its GMV during its IPO, it is already less than its peers and is still reducing. The company has focused more on gaining market share by spending money and acquiring customers rather than deriving value from its existing customers. I have borrowed the data from my mentor to showcase to you the vast amount of difference between Paytm and its peers.
- The second is that for a very long time, Paytm has not been able to generate profits and is not able to explain how and when they will earn profits. During a recent interview, I saw that they are keen on expanding their services which they are providing and not focusing on profitability. Even though the founders initially raised valuation, they needed to show profitability in business at some point in their life. Currently, as the business has increased, its operating losses have also increased and do not look sustainable. I expect it to become profitable after 6-7 years and have an operating profit margin of approx. 10% as it has started small finance lending to merchants. While constantly lending, they can earn greater margins from it as well as a huge amount of data which will be accumulated will lead to lower NPAs and reduced cost while lending to the merchants.

- In case of reinvestments, I assume that it will be able to generate Rs 3 for every Re 1 reinvested as in future, it will be able to derive more value from its existing customers and would not solely focus on expanding market share as well as the lending, which I explained in the earlier paragraph, would be one of the focal points. Considering this, its peers such as PayPal and Visa and are all able to earn around Rs 2.45 on every Re 1 invested and Rs 3 is because its competitors do not have anything like the lending facility. Ten years later, this advantage might not remain because of the competition as even new players are entering the market such as CRED.
- While there are certainly many risks, and as the company is growing, its ability to burn cash has been increasing, but since its IPO, the company has had a substantial cash balance, and therefore the probability of the company failing is kept to 5% only.

Valuation

If you think my Paytm story is good and you buy into the story, then you would believe that it will be able to grow its GMV by 40% CAGR for the next five years and will remain a market leader in its P2M market. Its loan book will also grow to expand its profits. Below I have given a snapshot of my story.

I have an understanding that many will disagree with the story that I have put here, and there will be some who will be telling me that I have not taken into consideration the proper valuation of all the acquisitions and mergers it had done to enhance its valuation, plus even Vijay Sharma might not agree to such lower valuation that I have come up to.

Paytm						Apr-22
The Story						
Paytm will continue its dominance of the Indian mobile payment market, while that market continues to grow. Along the way, its management will focus more on converting transactions on its platform into revenues, and revenues into operating income.						
The Assumptions						
	Base year	*Next year*	*Years 2-5*	*Years 6-10*	*After year 10*	*Link to story*
GMV	₹ 6,00,000	40.00%	40.00% →	4.00%	4.00%	Growing mobile payment market
Revenue as % of GMV	0.59%	0.67%	1.00% →	2.00%	2.00%	Take rate improves, as company matures
Operating margin (b)	-154.68%	-50.0%	-18.50% →	13.00%	13.00%	High-margin intermediary business
Tax rate	23.00%		25.00% →	25.00%	25.00%	Converge on statutory tax rate
Reinvestment (c)		1.50	3.00 →	3.00	40.00%	Industry average reinvestment, for capital intensive business.
Return on capital	-111.34%	Marginal ROIC =	50.71%		10.00%	Competitive advantages fade over time.
Cost of capital (d)			10.31% →	8.72%	8.72%	Cost of capital relatively stable.

The Cash Flows

	GMV	*Revenues*	*Operating Margin*	*EBIT (1-t)*	*Reinvestment*	*FCFF*
1	₹ 8,40,000	₹ 5,668.32	-50.00%	₹ -2,834.16	₹ 1,404.88	₹ -4,239.04
2	₹ 11,76,000	₹ 8,891.74	-37.40%	₹ -3,325.51	₹ 1,074.47	₹ -4,399.98
3	₹ 16,46,400	₹ 13,786.95	-31.10%	₹ -4,287.74	₹ 1,631.74	₹ -5,919.48
4	₹ 23,04,960	₹ 21,175.67	-24.80%	₹ -5,251.57	₹ 2,462.90	₹ -7,714.47
5	₹ 32,26,944	₹ 32,269.44	-18.50%	₹ -5,969.85	₹ 3,697.92	₹ -9,667.77
6	₹ 42,85,382	₹ 51,424.58	-12.20%	₹ -6,273.80	₹ 6,385.05	₹ -12,658.85
7	₹ 53,82,439	₹ 75,354.15	-5.90%	₹ -4,445.89	₹ 7,976.52	₹ -12,422.42
8	₹ 63,72,808	₹ 1,01,964.93	0.40%	₹ 407.86	₹ 8,870.26	₹ -8,462.40
9	₹ 70,86,563	₹ 1,27,558.13	6.70%	₹ 8,546.39	₹ 8,531.07	₹ 15.33
10	₹ 73,70,025	₹ 1,47,400.50	13.00%	₹ 19,162.07	₹ 6,614.13	₹ 12,547.94
Terminal year	₹ 76,64,826	₹ 1,53,296.52	13.00%	₹ 14,946.41	₹ 5,978.56	₹ 8,967.85

The Value

Terminal value	₹ 1,89,996.75		
PV(Terminal value)	₹ 74,388.80		
PV (CF over next 10 years)	₹ -35,358.85		
Value of operating assets =	₹ 39,029.95		
Adjustment for distress	₹ 975.75	Probability of failure =	5.00%
- Debt & Minority Interests	₹ 3,342.00		
+ Cash & Other Non-operating assets	₹ 8,925.00		
+IPO Proceeds	₹ 4,300.00		
Value of equity	₹ 47,937.20		
- Value of equity options	₹ 7,936.10		
Number of shares	62.43		
Value per share	₹ 640.70	Stock was trading at =	₹ 599.05

Image Source: Data made out from the assumptions

In my defense, maybe I might be wrong, and it might even be profitable sooner than I expect and grow GMV at a much faster rate or may go down while I expect it to remain the market leader in the P2M segment. Well, this valuation is based on my expectations from the company and to put it simply, you can create your own story and come up with different valuations.

Talking about the traditional one

Now let me talk about LIC which has been there in the business since even before I was born. I valued the company when its IPO came so you will also understand how to think about the company when IPO comes.

Let me start talking about the market details first and then we will move on to other segments.

Market

In the life insurance business, India is ranked tenth in the world. India's share in global life insurance was just 2.73% in 2019 and a mere 0.79% in the non-life insurance business in the same fiscal year, even though with such a small share, the industry has seen a growth of 9.63% in life insurance whereas globally the growth percentage comes only to 1.18% compared to the previous year.

If we compare it with other countries or if we wish to compare it globally, there are two metrics used for comparison.

- Insurance penetration
- Insurance density

Insurance Penetration can be measured as a percentage of insurance premiums to GDP and density is measured as a ratio of premiums to population. It can also be seen as per capita premium which as consumers we pay. Globally the insurance penetration is 3.35% with a density of USD 379. In comparison, the Indian scenario insurance penetration has increased from 2.71% to 3.76% from FY 2011-19.

Even though the increment is very low, we have witnessed this growth for the last 5-6 years only, because the government is trying to make the unorganised sector into an organised sector, as well as the improvement in the automobile industry. Even other factors played a vital role in the increase of the insurance industry, such as Covid-19 which played a vital role in making people realise, why it is so important to have insurance as well as advancements in the finance sector, improved digitisation, smartphone penetration, internet accessibility and the government schemes, all these things complemented each other simultaneously.

Offer for Sale

There are three things which are mentioned in the offer for sale. Firstly, the LIC is coming out with 316 mn shares to be available for the investors to invest in, out of which 5% is reserved for employees and 10% for policyholders who have linked their policy with their PAN. Many have rushed getting PAN linked after getting to know this information. Something which I didn't like in this offer for sale is that whole proceeds will be taken by the government to cover up their deficits and nothing will be left for LIC.

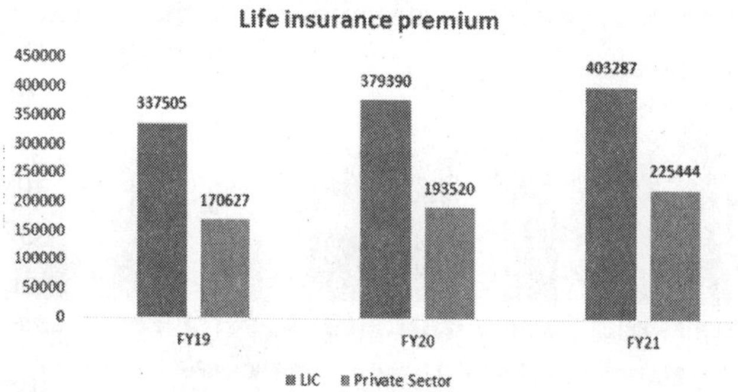

Image Source: LIC Financial statements

If you look at the above picture you will understand the mammoth share it has in the market and the number of insurance premiums it sold over the last three years from FY19-21. Few favourable drivers are playing a role in the increase in insurance premiums it sold.

- Favourable Demographics: This is one of the main reasons for it because of the younger population and the rise in nuclear families.
- Government programs: Government initiatives such as Pradhan Mantri Jan Arogya Yojana, Jeevan Jyoti Beema Yojana and many other initiatives.
- Automobile Industry: Strong demand for personal mobility vehicles leading to increased demand for insurance.
- Growing household savings: Increased formalisation of savings in the households and increasing awareness towards the financial instruments available for savings.
- Heavy Marketing: Not only by the government but even the private companies and the startups like Policybazaar etc.

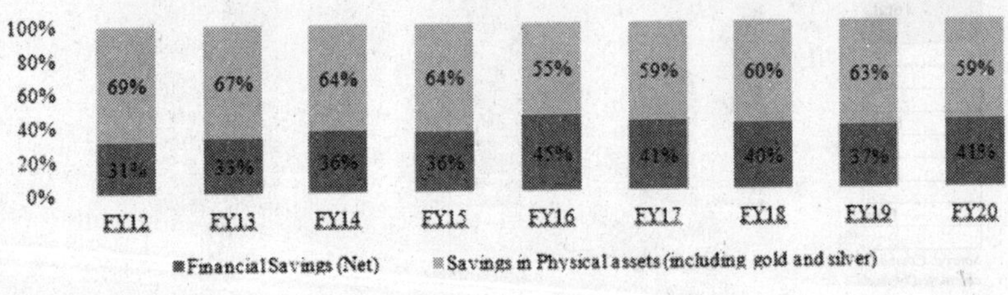

Image Source: LIC Financial Statements

Even though I told you that there is increasing household savings in financial products, the graph tells you how much increment is there. Fun fact, according to CRISIL research, only 27% are financially literate or know about the financial products that are there in the market for them to make savings.

Financials

Now, the main thing that I wanted to talk about which will help you decide whether to invest in this company or not –

BENCHMARKING AGAINST TOP INDIAN PRIVATE LIFE INSURERS

Market share of LIC, top 5 private players and other players[1] in the industry (as of Fiscal Year 2021)

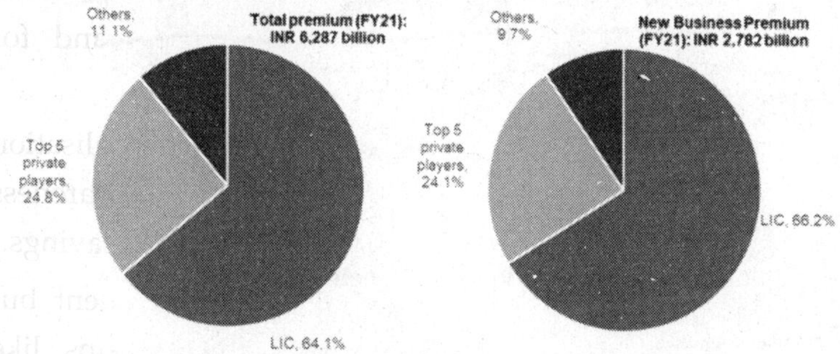

Source: Company public disclosures, CRISIL Research

Note: [1]Other players include 18 private players operating in the industry as of Fiscal Year 2021

Total Premium – FY21	Total Premium (INR billion)	Customer Mix (Basis total premium)	
		Individual	Group
LIC	4,032.9	66.5%	33.5%
SBI Life	502.5	81.7%	18.3%
HDFC Life	385.8	73.7%	26.3%
ICICI Prudential Life	357.3	85.2%	14.8%
Max Life	190.2	96.8%	3.2%
Bajaj Allianz Life	120.2	68.3%	31.7%
Others	698.3	86.3%	13.7%
Private players total	2,254.3	83.9%	16.1%
Total	6,287.3	72.6%	27.4%

Source: Company public disclosures, Life Insurance Council (New Business Performance), CRISIL Research Note: The customer mix data is calculated basis data disclosed by the players in L-36 schedule on premium paying policies

Image Source: LIC Financial statements

This is a screenshot taken from the draft they have filed with SEBI. I am very happy to look at the market share of LIC; no other industry has such a vast difference, even Asian Paints does not have such a huge difference with the competitors. This clearly shows that it has market dominance and a monopoly type situation where even when inflation is rising, LIC can keep the price the same and can squeeze the profits out of competitors.

Total Cost Ratio (as % of total premium)

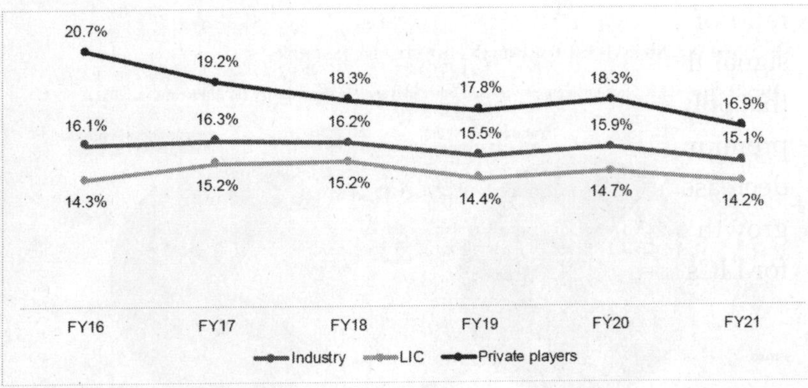

Source: IRDAI, CRISIL Research
Note: Total Cost = Commission + Operating Expense

Image Source: LIC Financial statements

LIC has been able to keep the cost steady as a percentage of total premiums, so we can assume that it has a better supply chain and management than other private players. It also comes to me as a concern that private players have been reducing and getting better and better with their total cost ratio. Soon, there might be a time that they have the same ratio as LIC or even less and this thing can create problems with LIC not being able to match the cost with a possibility of losing market share in future. Even though it is such a big organisation, it is losing market share and its share came down from 66.4% to 64.10%.

Another concern is that it is not able to grow as fast as the private players. While the private players grew at a pace of 18% CAGR, LIC has grown only by 9% CAGR when we talk about the life insurance industry. LICs persistency ratio was 79% in 2021 for the thirteenth month, it still lags behind its peers such as SBI Life and HDFC Life which had a persistency ratio of 88% and 90% respectively. This clearly gives me a signal that people are not paying premiums, or we can say that only 79% of people who are buying insurance are paying premiums. In a market where even a slight drop in profits or decrease in revenues is being punished by investors, the low growth and low persistency ratio are definitely detrimental for LICs' future earnings.

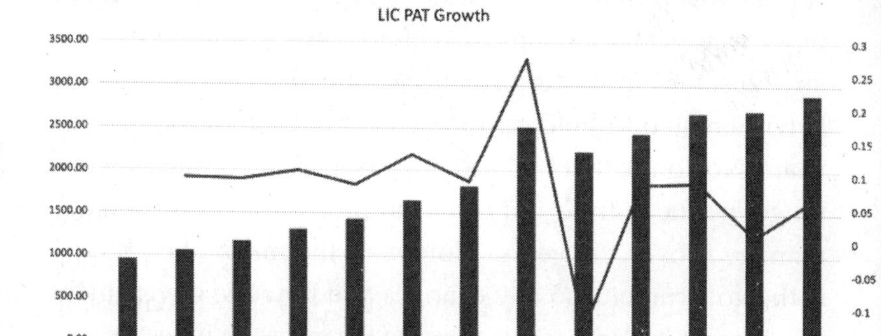

	Mar-2009	Mar-2010	Mar-2011	Mar-2012	Mar-2013	Mar-2014	Mar-2015	Mar-2016	Mar-2017	Mar-2018	Mar-2019	Mar-2020	Mar-2021
PAT	957.35	1060.72	1171.80	1313.34	1437.59	1656.68	1823.78	2517.85	2231.74	2446.40	2688.50	2712.71	2900.57
PAT Growth		9.75%	9.48%	10.78%	8.64%	13.22%	9.16%	27.57%	-12.82%	8.77%	9.00%	0.89%	6.48%

Data Source: LIC DRHP, Ace Equity, Own Research

As mentioned earlier in this segment that our industry has grown more over the last 5-6 years, you can see the performance impact where there is very low or uneven growth in the profit after tax.

There is another metric that you should know, called Value of New Business (VNB). VNB is the present value of all the business an insurer underwrites in a year and can be loosely compared to PAT.

If I compare VNB with its peers, the latest data shows that its VNB margin was only 9.3%, which means that it is operating on thin margins, whereas companies like HDFC Life and SBI Life has a margin of 24.4% and 21.8%. Also, this tells you that its competitors have enough space to even provide offers and their advancement with the help of IT has helped them keep good margins, which LIC has failed to do even with such good cashflows. There were articles regarding ROCE of LIC being eighty-three times, but the amount of capital was different and what shall I do with ROCE if the other factors are not aligned with increasing it, nor do I find any reason from its performance or the discussion as to how it will be able to hold its market dominance in the coming years. No doubt, that LIC will hold its market dominance for a longer period of time, but I have no clarity as to how they will manage it over the years. Moreover, the major shareholder is the government, so any changes and how the government might react is also a major concern for me as an investor.

You might remember when the government said that it will take 50% of the convenience fees from the IRCTC and the market value of IRCTC immediately eroded. We don't know what will happen to LIC or even something like this may happen or not.

Conclusion

Even though LIC might be in business from a longer period of time than its peers, it seems to me that LIC would not be able to hold its market share. That's because while looking at all these metrics it seems to me that private companies are competing better and would be able to provide me better growth when it comes to compounding. You can also create a story and try and do it yourself and identify whether you wish to invest in a company or not.

You must understand that metrics which are not the financial metrics should be subjective and should provide you a range rather than an absolute number and should be able to help you put numbers to a story which makes sense. If you just put numbers for the sake of it, then it won't make you believe in that investment that company which you just valued on your own.

Now coming to the second topic which I mentioned above – the Hockey Stick approach[56] which businesses use.

56 This part is from the learnings of McKinsey report which I read during studying this approach.

Hockey Stick Approach

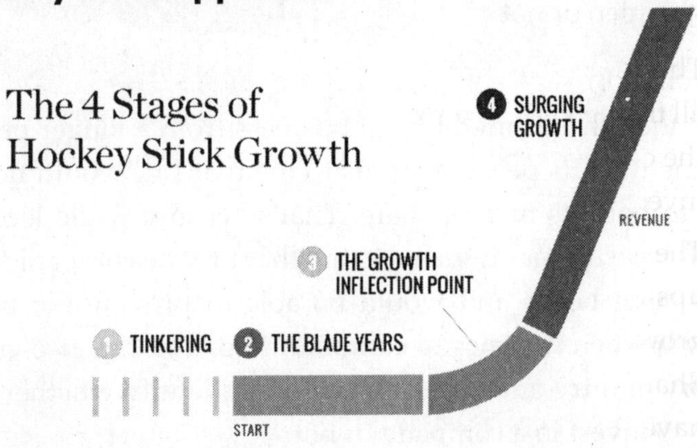

Image Source: copper.com

1. The first stage is the tinkering stage, wherein the entrepreneurs focus more on their start-up ideas and make plans, business models, and strategies they would pursue. Even though in these years, they might not be fully committed to the product or idea, but are testing it working part-time on their current idea.
2. The blade years generally comprise 3-4 years of time wherein they focus on funding, and the partners or entrepreneurs are pursuing the idea or venture on a full-time basis, with the promise made to the investors that if they have capital now and invest those now by even giving discounts, they have a bright future ahead of their profitability, as well as revenue would start coming in. A similar case to what Reliance did with its Jio platforms wherein they give data on a free basis for a year and then started asking for revenue, and now they are the market

leader as well as having a good amount of profits, where the other telecom sectors are struggling.

3. The inflection point is where the magic happens, wherein all the market penetration strategy that is being used and the capital they have received result in growth driven by invested capital.
4. The last phase is the surging revenues which many start-ups are able to get, either based on organic or inorganic growth. Companies such as Zomato, Paytm, PhonePe, BharatPe and many other listed and unlisted start-ups have revenue surges, but fail to accomplish the promise of profitability which was shown to the investors. They also fail to accomplish the revenue targets which they have shown to investors. If we look at the recent failures, we can see that Zomato has failed to accomplish even the revenue targets wherein now Swiggy controls the majority of the market share, and even the take rate that Zomato has is decreasing because of the deep discounts they continue to offer in order to retain the consumers and the heavy advertising.

While the basis of this approach starts with promises which are made to get investment now, which would generate good returns after a few years, it fails because of the biasness regarding the things which are beyond the control of the investor/entrepreneur.

Not mentioning Reliance Jio, which has excelled in this strategy, let us talk about the bleeding unicorns which have just raised valuation and have failed to deliver on the promises made.

The first is the overconfidence of the baseline, meaning they have confidence that because there is investment coming through, they are going to generate x amount of returns. They fail because the acceptance of the product is in the hands of consumers. When we look at the majority of start-ups, they are consumer-facing businesses. Thus, the end result of the business as to whether they are willing to pay the price for the value that the business has provided remains in the hands of consumers, as well as the macro factors which keep on affecting the daily lives of the consumers. Now assume that there is recession coming up and a banking or an NBFC says that it would grow its loan book by 10-15%. It would be very difficult to digest such scenario because the cost of capital for majority of the businesses would increase, the customers would be precautioned whether to spend more and the businesses would not thinking of investing CAPEX because the demand will be decreasing and there would be job cuts when recession fears are there. This is known as overestimation of baseline.

The second is the timidity in the execution of the business plan. The majority of the start-ups have become so large that they need a minimum amount of cash flow in order to sustain themselves and many of them are dependent on large advertising budgets, which increases the customer acquisition costs. And whenever the funding goes down, there is a decrease in the active consumer which can be seen in their financial statements. When you compare FMCG companies such as Mamaearth, which is a private company, and a company like HUL, both of them are having distribution channels, both the companies are having similar kinds of products, but still HUL is able to take better margins and has lower cost of customer acquisition when compared to Mamaearth – which focuses solely on marketing and that too majority of the marketing is done through online channels which eventually increases the cost of acquiring customers.

In majority of the cases, 90% of the time, only one business lifts the whole company. Such as, in Reliance, the refinery business is the cash cow. In Tata Group, it is TCS and so on. Even in terms of economic profits, large businesses which perform uniquely in the market take the majority of the market share.

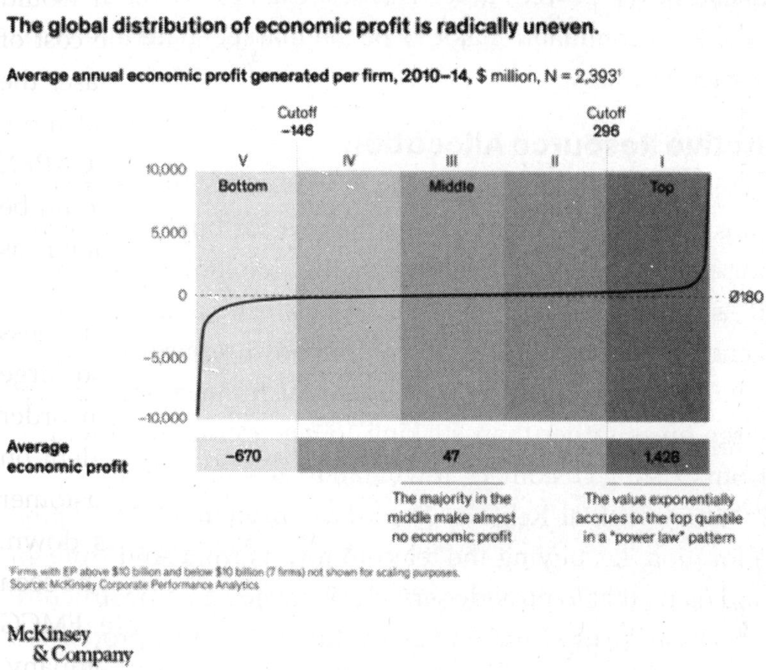

Image Source: McKinsey & Company

The above image showcases distribution of economic profits as to how top 20% of the companies take majority of the economic profits globally.

The success and failure of this model depends on the five elements which I have learnt[57] and even have observed in the markets while studying companies and their business models. While investing in any company, the power curve (image above) shows that not all companies or even industries would be able to move up the power curve. There would be few declining industries and few new age industries such as renewables. Companies in renewables might be able to move ahead in the power curve. The best example is Tesla, which is able to command majority of the market share in electric vehicles in USA.

Active Resource Allocation

While capital budgeting decision plays a significant role in most businesses, many companies go for buybacks, which raises the shareholder returns or the shareholder valuation. It is finally raising the EPS of the firm and eventually generating better returns. If the company uses its resources in a haphazard manner or like butter which can be spread over large areas rather than sticking to generating more returns from existing customers, it will fail to generate profits.

If we look at Reliance Jio, it has wisely made its capital allocation, i.e. buying the telecom towers from Anil Ambani and using that to provide services; it created an infrastructure which can be used and will give returns in a better proportion

57 Chris Bradley, 2019

than the advertisement. It also bought GTPL, Den Networks and Hathaway to foray into cable and broadcasting manner which were already into profits.

On the other hand, if we look at Zomato and Paytm, they have made acquisitions which were already into losses and kept on adding new markets without becoming a market leader, which is efficient and is a cash cow in a particular business segment. Also, companies like Zomato and Paytm struggle to derive better value from the existing customers because they need to offer discounts to the consumers. Failing which, the consumer might shift to another company.

Strong Capital Programs

Companies such as Reliance, Asian Paints, Pidilite and many more have strong capital programs, i.e. they can utilise their resources more efficiently and grow faster than the industry growth. Their ratio of capital to sales exceeds their peers, which in turn showcases their capital budgeting decisions. Companies like Pidilite have invested in expanding their markets. If you think that Pidilite is just Fevicol, those days are gone because Fevicol only accounts to 20-25% of their total business. They have added other areas of construction chemicals which are used while building the house.

Distinctive Productivity Improvements

All these companies that have successfully implemented the hockey stick approach have been consistently focusing on productivity improvements made by them and are the best in the industry according to the industry standards. Either they have improved by bringing software which can do demand forecasting or by improving supply chain management, or removing the unnecessary businesses which were not profitable. Asian paints realised that there is need for paints of different colours. Paint shops have small shelves in India, and there is not so much space available with the store owner. What they did was they invested in a super computer in 1970 and started forecasting demand. They even developed a machine which was placed with the store owners.

Here what the machine had was few inks of different colours which could be mixed with the base colour to create the shade which the customer wants. The waiting time for customer was reduced from 3-4 days to 2-3 mins and thus was able to capture the market. It is not the best quality paint you will find in the market, but it understood the customer's pain point and delivered according to it.

Differentiation Improvement

This is necessary as in order to gain market share and customers paying you; there is a need to improve or innovate the products, services and even business models. If you look at Page Industries, it has brought in demand forecasting software known as Blue Yonder which has helped in reducing the dead stock with the distributors and lowering SKUs as well as they have started investing in exclusive Jockey stores, which provides a different experience than most of its peers.

Programmatic M&As

Mergers and Acquisitions are part and parcel of business. You are wrong if you think that M&As don't provide synergy in the business. It provides a certain kind of synergy, but then M&A decisions should be considering the market share which you have and what the company is going to provide in future. Again, discussing the companies in which I have invested, companies such as Asian paints, Pidilite, GMM Pfaudler have all done acquisitions when required and then increased or expanded to new markets. If I again talk about Asian paints, it has invested in a company called Sleek, which is involved in home décor items or you can say interior design and is providing kitchen appliances. They are earning well and there's a double digit growth. When you look at the ecommerce space, the players are fighting over price and nothing more has changed in that. It might change in the coming years for the new age tech companies because they are able to provide a good customer experience through their front end.

Let me explain how things are going to change with the ecommerce space in the next segment. There are two things which are going to happen.

1. OCEN: Open Credit Enablement Network
2. ONDC: Open Network for Digital Commerce

Both the things are products of India Stack.

OCEN

You must be wondering what India Stack is by looking at the image. India stack is a stack of open-source protocols that private companies can use to benefit Indian consumers. You can see the image which represents how different layers of protocols are created which can be used by any company to use in their business.

India Stack	What is it?	What is in it?	Who is the owner?
Consent layer	A modern privacy data sharing framework	Open personal data store	Reserve Bank of India
Cashless layer	An electronic interoperable payment network	IMPS, AEPS,APB, UPI	National Payments Corporation of India
.Paperless layer	Easily store and retrieve information digitally	Aadhaar e-KYC, e-Sign, Digital Locker	Department of Electronics and Information Technology
Presence-less layer	Unique digital biometric identity with open API access	Aadhaar card, Mobile Aadhaar	Unique Identification Authority of India

Image Source: Indiastack.org

Image Source: Indiastack.org

As you know that we are brewing financialization ahead, it all started in 2013 when Nandan Nilekani came out with his brainchild, the Aadhaar system. We all at the time of starting didn't know that it would play out to be very big, but it turned out to be even better than our expectations.

Nowhere in the world except India, we can do e-signs such as signing a legal document which can be accepted anywhere is possible through the cloud. For example, if you are signing your rental agreement which has been sent to you by your landlord, you can sign it with the help of Aadhaar validation and once it is validated the sign is also considered validated.

I don't need to explain the payment method of UPI, we all know it is such a huge success, wherein with the help of QR codes, we all can make payments.

We all have UPI, IMPS, NEFT and even RTGS. Then where will OCEN come into play?

Over quite a few years, banks are trying to find a solution for lending, wherein in the traditional lending scenario, the banks or the NBFCs can give you loans on your collateral or based on credit history. But what about those who have not taken loans or consumers who don't have collateral to provide?

This is where India Stack came up with the solution of democratising the whole lending sector economy. What used to happen is that the banks provided loans to safe consumers or businesses while the MSMEs not having collateral, or a credit history used to get loans at a higher rate of interest and some MSMEs didn't even get the loans. It is estimated that around 300 bn dollars' worth of lending is missed because of all these things.

What OCEN is trying to do is that in a similar fashion to ONDC, it will be having multiple layers.

- LSP (loan service providers)
  - Account Aggregators

- Lenders
- Consumers

Setting the table

Traditionally, lenders used to send their agents who would do all the work and acquire customers, do KYC, and bring different information from the consumers and provide it to the companies.

Here, the scenario is going to change. Just imagine Zomato or Swiggy which are the two largest food delivery and food review platforms, they become a Loan Service Providers. Both Swiggy and Zomato can provide loans to restaurants for the restaurants to expand or function on daily basis.

How can this be possible? Right?

Assume that Zomato ties up with Bajaj Finance or any other NBFC or even a bank, anyone can come into the picture. What the banks used to do it is they needed certain information or collateral to give loans. Here the restaurants are already listed on Zomato and have done KYC, and Zomato also has certain kinds of data such as regular orders dispatched through Zomato and other stuff which might be useful for banks for assessment.

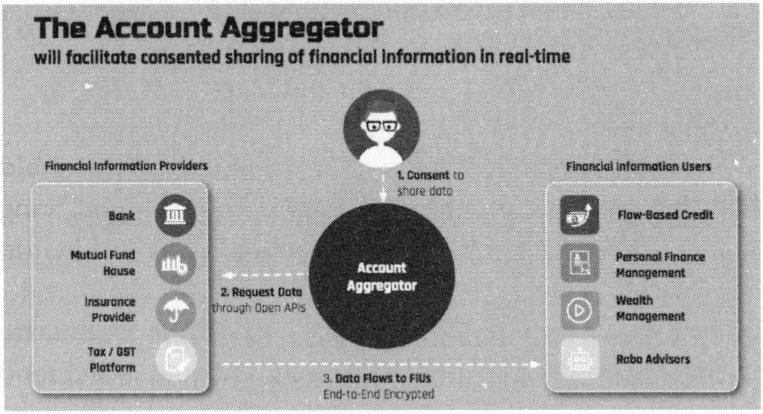

Image Source: indiastack.org

Now the account aggregator comes into the picture wherein his job is to bring information from various sources such as KYC details, UPI transaction details as well as other details provided by Zomato or Swiggy in a format that the bank requires to assess the information whether to give credit or not.

Lenders will be easily able to provide more lending and come up with customised solutions to provide it to the person taking the loan, as well as all this process reduces the cost of customer acquisition.

If you are just sticking to the restaurant business because I gave you an example and are not able to imagine a use case beyond that, you might be thinking about how a normal consumer can benefit.

Just imagine that Byjus or Vedantu or some edutech company becomes a loan service provider. Byjus would be having the data on how their student is performing, whether he/she has a good prospect of getting a job or even starting a business, and whether the student is performing well or badly. Byjus will be having all this data and even might predict based on a few metrics.

Let us assume that Byjus ties up with all the banks and NBFC and enables student loan facilities for its students. Here the account aggregator would again bring all the information needed for the bank and the bank might be able to come up with a customised solution which can be used by the student to take loan and the student can select, which offer he/she wants to take.

How does it solve the problem as many layers are added? Won't it be more complicated?

First, you need to understand that OCEN is an open API. How the companies use the open API of the UPI system, in the same manner, different companies such as HDFC Bank, Bajaj Finance, Big Basket, Zomato and name any company which you want – all these companies have their own APIs and if OCEN as an open API was not there, it would have been very difficult for these companies to integrate as for every integration, they would require different API in some or the other form.

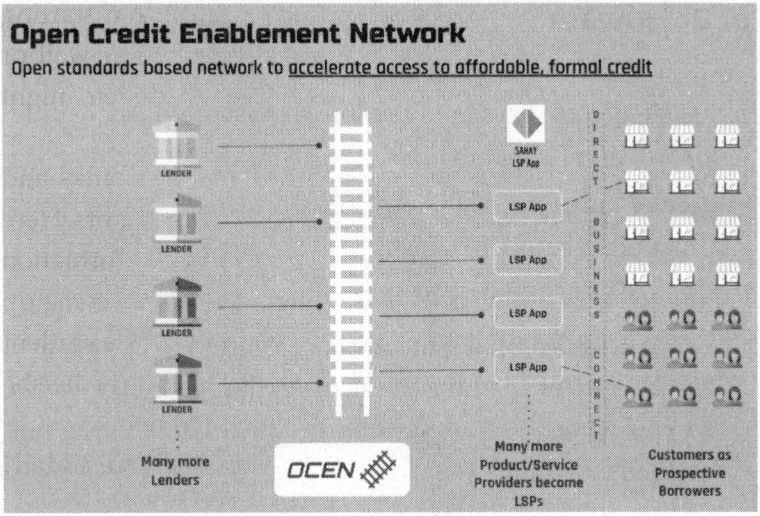

Image Source: indiastack.org

Since it is a single API, anybody can use this protocol and use it to collaborate with lenders or LSPs and provide services.

Now coming to the question as to what the benefit to the various parties is associated with the OCEN Network.

For Lenders

- As the lenders are enrolling on the protocol, they have access to the vast majority of pools of customers of different domains gathered by the LSPs.
- Customised offers can be made according to the consumer which earlier would have been difficult because of higher customer cost acquisition.
- Better monitoring of the consumer, because the consumer is sharing certain more data through the LSPs if any red flags can be monitored easily and steps can be taken to reduce NPAs.

For Borrowers

- Easy access to credit based on the past history of their usage of apps, not being relied on past credit score only or collateral to get loans.
- Lower interest rate probably because of reduced customer acquisition cost.
- Tailor-made offers by banks or other lending institutions.
- More transactional data being captured and not just credit card or loan data which might give better access to credit facilities of various products which was not available earlier.

For Loan Service Provider apps

- They might be able to have one more revenue stream from what they are currently earning, depending on the collaboration by the LSPs.
- More revenue out of the same consumer which would improve their margins.

Just to summarize

- Originations - LSP
- KYC - eKYC, PAN, Account Aggregator
- Underwriting - LSP, Account Aggregator
- Documentation - eSIGN
- Collections - LSP, eNACH, credit card, UPI e-mandate
- Monitoring - Account Aggregator
- Disbursals - NEFT, IMPS, RTGS, UPI

Conclusion

I have just imagined to use the case right now, I don't know what all better things can come, maybe as time passes even I will be able to understand the use cases better. As this thing is coming up which is new, similarly, we were just speculating during the time of UPI and now we can see the wonders it is making. We might just see the same in OCEN.

Now let me take you to the next big thing called ONDC.

ONDC

You might have heard in the news that ONDC is coming up or it will break the monopoly of the players like Amazon and Flipkart and will open up ways for new players who are struggling or the small shops who are struggling to get business online and are not able to get because of the big players and their discounts.

Yes, things are going to change a bit, but in a better way for all the players.

The intention

Similar to OCEN, ONDC is a protocol which will make and connect apps through its open APIs. The intention of the government was to democratize the whole ecommerce space and then a possibility that all the players in the ecommerce space would get equal opportunity and thus might increase their revenue shares as well as it would benefit the consumers as they will have the flexibility to choose from the vendor they wish to have. They will have the flexibility to choose from the logistics service provider they wish to have as well as from the app which they wish to order.

Currently what is happening is that the whole e-commerce environment is a closed environment. Let me explain! When you open Amazon, you are able to see only those products which are listed on their platform, then when you order from those products, the logistics partner is also decided by Amazon, and they need to be registered with Amazon. What the ONDC will do is every platform that is consumer facing platform such as Zomato, HDFC Bank App, Big Basket can be the seller and all these apps can have multiple things associated with them. Let me explain in detail how this will work by bifurcating the whole thing in buyer and seller platform.

Seller platform

Seller platform is the front side of the platform or the apps which the customers are going to use – apps such as Paytm, HDFC Bank app, Zomato, Big basket, Ola and many more. Technically any app which has a large customer base can be named as a seller app. Now as the government intends to democratize the whole buying experience, what you will be able to do is, if you want to book Ola, or even order food, you might not need two apps for doing different tasks.

You might like Paytm UI better than other apps, so you can search for a restaurant on Paytm app, and you will get a list of restaurants with their reviews which are posted there, and all the restaurants will be registered on the buyer app or platform and also decide which person should come to deliver you food. If the restaurant already has a tie-up, then there won't be a problem, but if not, then you can decide on the logistics partner.

Similarly, you can book a ride from Paytm app and decide which provider should come to pick you up. This would stand true for other apps also which are seller apps, meaning that every seller app will have the opportunity to provide every type of service which is there on buyer app.

Buyer platform

Any company can register themselves on the buyer platform or the buyer app. Assume that your nearby kirana store gets registered on the buyer app, then all the things which he owns in the shop will be listed as the inventory on the seller platform. He needs to register on just one platform and all those apps which are using the open protocol will also display the kirana shop's products. Similarly, even a large company such as BigBasket can register themselves on the buyer app. The reason they would do so is because even BigBasket will get access to multiple customers who were not earlier using it and the probability that it might be able to reduce its customer acquisition cost is heightened.

To summarise

Sellers who are selling something will have better reach because of being registered on multiple apps which the consumers are using and the consumer facing app such as Paytm, Zomato and others will have the potential to generate more revenue because they are able add more services to their platform.

10.
Principles

I have made lots of mistakes while investing in companies, and there were many times where I was not able to concentrate on long term vision, sometimes didn't have patience either while buying or selling and sometimes even valued the company based on the price and just sold it on the same day without thinking anything because of the information overload that happens to every individual.

Thus, to minimize losses and even make few mistakes, I have developed few principles which I stick to.

Invest for long term

I always think about investing for a longer period of time. As I have already mentioned that I have a time frame of thirty years. What many investors forget is that we are ultimately investing in a business, and business will take time to give results. In Gujarat, we have a saying that we need to give at least 1000 days to the business, and then the business will take care of the owner.

Similarly, if we look at daily price actions of the stock, we are not going to get results, but if you give business 3-4 years and even more, as many as possible, then it will show you proper returns. It is, as Warren Buffet says in many interviews, that if you have a piece of land and you look at the land the next day and keep doing that over a few days, nothing is going to happen; the land is suddenly not growing or decreasing or giving fruits.

You will need to wait for a few seasons to see multiple crops and get the taste of the fruits you have sowed.

Behaviour is everything

It takes behaviour and discipline to control ourselves. One of the things I do is not look at the stock prices on a daily basis; instead, I just understand what is going on in the market and read and watch the news. I don't even look at the quarterly performance of the stock but just read the annual financial statement.

There is so much information overload going on nowadays that there are chances that I can make mistakes; therefore, I restrict myself from watching daily stock market prices because nowadays, buying and selling a stock is just at our fingertips. We open the app and either swipe left or right, and then it is done.

On the other hand, suppose you purchase a piece of land and then, after a few years, you wish to sell it. It will take time; first, you need to find the buyer at the price you wish to sell, and then even after finding the buyer, you will get the payments not within a day or two but in some months. Therefore, taking time and while you think of all these things, you might even change your decision to sell the land.

Moderation/Diversified Portfolio

You already know this principle. From diversification point it may be different industries which are not totally correlated or even if they are, then having few companies with different weightage.

Imagine if you had invested in Future Retail stock and had other stocks also on an equal weightage basis; you would have been saved if you exited even at losses. You know what happened to Future Retail.

Risk and Reward Understanding

There has to be absolute clarity on this. You do not invest the amount which you require in the near future, and that too on riskier instruments. It is better to understand our risk appetite for investing in particular stocks. It is not always that only high-risk stocks will give you better rewards. The stocks which have been performing consistently well will also make you rich.

One of the risks and reward things that many new-age investors get trapped in is thinking about getting rich quickly. Unless and until you are speculating just to understand and that too, investing very less capital is okay, but investing the main principal amount wherein you might suffer a reduction in the principal amount is madness.

Spending less than you earn

Many of us fail to make a budget or a financial plan for ourselves, and then we might need cash on an immediate basis and would need to dilute our investments either on loss or even if it was on profit, the real return would be less, as I have explained earlier. We in India have the habit of saving, so I don't need to explain the benefits of this principle to you.

Leveraging Kills

Never invest money by taking loans of a certain kind and invest that money in the stock market. Taking loans for business is good for growing the business, but taking loans to invest in the stock market is foolishness. Firstly, you will always think of profit booking as you also need to pay interest, and none of us has the ability to time the markets and is sure that we will get certain amounts of returns.

There can be a time when the markets are giving negative returns or even if they are positive, the returns might be less than the rate of interest and the interest you need to pay.

Understand how you invest

It is always better to stick to a method of investing; just because there are many financial experts in the market saying all sorts of things. You need to cut out that noise and understand your style of investing, but sometimes you need to challenge your beliefs and check whether they are still valid or not.

You might have heard that having fewer companies, around ten companies, will give you better returns than having 25-30 companies. There is no such proven thing; Peter Lynch, at a given point in life, invested in 1400 companies and was still beating the market. On the other hand, we have Warren Buffet, who has made investments in a few limited companies, which he understands. Similarly, if you look at mutual funds, there are generally 10-20 companies.

Why many investors say that investing in fewer companies is good – there is a limitation to the understanding of different sectors, and the fund manager also cannot track 30-40 companies, it will be a nightmare for the manager if such situation happens for an individual person.

Be aware of your own limitations

We all have different ideologies and mindsets, which help us perform in a certain way and make decisions accordingly. Thus, you need to also understand your limitations and take help from wherever possible.

For example, I do not understand the pharma industry, so I avoid investing in it and even advising on that topic. Also, as the block chain was a new concept, I took time and help to understand the technology and then decided whether to invest in it or not.

Be responsible

You need to take responsibility for every decision you make while investing in the stock markets. If you exit from the market at a loss because you require money to invest in real estate, you need to be responsible for that. If you were investing in a penny stock and invested a few thousand, speculating that it will give you 20-25% returns and lose all your money, you need to take responsibility for that. You cannot blame any other person when you invest in the wrong company, which might go bankrupt, and then blame the person who suggested you. No one made it compulsory.

You also need to take responsibility when you gain from the investment you made because it was the right judgement which you took after rejecting many companies.

Prepare for crisis

You always need to be ready for a crisis. It might come at any time. For preparing for a crisis, you might have different investments or even insurances which would help you in difficult times or even reduce or recover any losses which you might suffer because of the losses.

Invest in yourself

Investing in yourself is the best investment you can make. Reading and learning as well as acquiring new skills even if it is just for investing, you will become a better investor when you learn different things. You will become smarter than what you are right now.

References

https://auto.hindustantimes.com/auto/news/indias-first-indigenously-developed-hydrogen-fuel-cell-bus-unveiled-in-pune-41661142207167.html

https://www.reuters.com/business/energy/india-plans-produce-5-mln-tonnes-green-hydrogen-by-2030-2022-02-17/

https://lightson.news/c/indias-place-in-the-new-hydrogen-world-order

https://www.jdpower.com/cars/shopping-guides/whats-the-difference-between-gray-blue-and-green-hydrogen

https://www.tata.com/about-us/tata-group-our-heritage

https://www.itcportal.com/sustainability/index.aspx

https://www.bseindia.com/publicissue.html

https://economictimes.indiatimes.com/markets/commodities/news/what-led-crude-oil-prices-fall-below-0-a-barrel/articleshow/75264813.cms?from=mdr

https://www.fortuneindia.com/enterprise/godrej-family-split-vikhroli-land-the-bone-of-contention/106130

https://investorzone.in/buyback/tcs-buyback-2022/

https://www.businesstoday.in/markets/company-stock/story/ambuja-cements-adani-enterprises-acc-shares-rise-347564-2022-09-19

https://www.financialexpress.com/market/adani-enterprises-acc-ambuja-cements-share-prices-tank-over-7-after-share-pledge-by-adani-group/2681610/

https://www.mckinsey.com/business-functions/strategy-and-corporate-finance/our-insights/how-to-make-the-bold-strategy-moves-that-matter